JOYFUL IN HOPE

Cardinal Eduardo F. Pironio

JOYFUL
IN HOPE

St Paul Publications

Original title: *Lieti nella Speranza,* Edizioni Paoline, Roma.
Translated from the Italian by Kent White, M.A.

The Scripture quotations in this publication are from the Revised Standard Version Bible, Catholic Edition, copyrighted © 1965 and 1966 by the Division of Christian Education of the National Council of the Churches of Christ in the U.S.A., and used by permission.

St Paul Publications
Middlegreen, Slough SL3 6BT

Copyright © Edizioni Paoline, Roma, 1978
English translation copyright © St Paul Publications 1979

Nihil obstat: M. J. Byrnes, ssp, stl.
Imprimatur: F. Diamond, vg, Northampton, Sept. 25, 1979

First published in Great Britain November 1979
Reprinted March 1980.
Printed by the Society of St Paul, Slough

ISBN 085439 156 8

St Paul Publications is an activity of the priests and brothers of the Society of St Paul who promote the christian message through the mass media.

CONTENTS

DEDICATION

It is a commonplace that the religious life is in a state of crisis and at a turning point, as are the church, civil society, the family . . .

There is a very great need of optimism and hope, not springing from any human cause, but rather from the joyful certainty that if Christ dies, it is for three days! Then comes the Resurrection! Prophets, preachers and witnesses arise to show us the way in this juncture.

Innumerable consecrated people (and not only they!) will wish quietly to read over and over again the message of a witness for the "Resurrection of Christ" living in this age of ours: may his proclamation, echoing in their hearts, become a spur to "conversion" and to "action".

These twelve articles, some of them already published elsewhere, are offered by the Author in a collection which has been made with special love and is guaranteed to be an authentic and definitive edition.

May it be presented to Christ and to the consecrated, by the poor and contemplative Virgin, the handmaid of the Lord and the Mother of God and of humankind.

JOYFUL IN HOPE

> Rejoice in your hope, be patient in tribulation, be constant in prayer (Rom 12:12).

I. I wish to be a pastor

WHEN I learnt — at a most unexpected time — that Paul VI was entrusting me with the care of those who live consecrated lives, I said to myself: "I must continue to be a pastor; the only thing I have to give to the religious, apart from an ardent love for the church, is the sincere love I bear for them, and the wish to be of use to them as an instrument of the Spirit".

How am I to work with them and for them if I do not fully share their crosses and their hopes, their sufferings in their search for God and the deep joy of their daily faithfulness? I think that I should visit them and write to them in order to be in constant touch with them so as to listen to, direct and encourage them. I wish to be a pastor, a pastor who intends to know his flock by experience, to give them the life of Christ and to live in the great joy of fellowship with them all in the Spirit (Jn 10:11-16).

In my first visit to the Holy Father after my appointment, he said to me "I know that you are feeling very sad, and that for two reasons: for what you have left behind, and for the cross which I have laid upon your shoulders. Yes, it is indeed a heavy one, but we will bear it together. And I may add that you have to deal with a privileged part of the church: the consecrated life. Not only so, but I dare to promise you that soon you will find that it brings you great happiness". And, in truth, it does.

I am happy because I have said YES to the Lord with all my heart. I am happy to be working so closely in conjunction with the Holy Father. But I am happy above all because my service in the universal church now consists in enlivening the consecrated life of religious and of secular institutes, and that precisely in this time of opportunity for the church and for the world.

II. Witnesses of Easter

I write my first message for Easter; with the simplicity and love of a father, a brother, a friend. The message is bound to be a cry of hope: "It is true! The Lord has risen ... and has appeared to Simon" (Lk 23:34).

Religious are by definition, witnesses of the kingdom, a kingdom which is already among us in Jesus Christ (Mt 1:15) and is to be fully realised in the Parousia (1 Cor 15:19-28). Every Christian is a witness of Easter, and therefore has received the Spirit of power (Ac 1:8). But, in the church, the bishops "the priests who help him" (LG 21) and the religious have the mission of proclaiming to the world the coming of a kingdom of truth, righteousness and love. As witnesses of a Christ who has died and is risen, they call to repentance for the remission of sins (Lk 24:46-48). At Easter all religious are bound to live in deep contemplation, in the serenity of the cross and in generous giving to the brethren.

"Be joyful in hope" (Rom 12:12) is the heritage, the obligation and the message for all religious. It is an invitation for all who have been baptised. Yet, obviously, it is of special concern to those who, by a special consecration, have made a fundamental choice of the Christ of Easter. It is not a matter of simply living in joy, but, fundamentally, of passing on the joy of the kingdom to all the brethren. It is not a matter of simply living quietly in hope, but rather, for everybody, of being turned into fervent and shining prophets of that hope.

Today's world needs this daily witness of simple souls who, united to Christ crucified, irradiate the Spirit and by his means to communicate to men and women the joy of salvation and the hope of the kingdom already begun. People of today suffer much; there is need to communicate joy, fruit of love and the Spirit, to them (Gal 5:22). The world at present is paralysed by pessimism and sorrow; we must cry to it: "The Lord is at hand" (Phil 4:5); we must proclaim that he is present and walking with us.

III. Witnesses and prophets

The religious must proclaim, with life and speech, this authentic testimony of the kingdom, the resurrection of Christ Jesus: "This Jesus God raised up, and of that we all are witnesses" (Acts 2:32). But it is above all the community which manifests his presence (AG 15) and by the power of the Spirit bears witness to Easter. The primitive community — united by the Spirit in the Word, the breaking of the bread and service to the brethren — lives "with glad and generous hearts, praising God and having favour with all the people" (Acts 2:42-47).

A genuine fraternal community — living in deep contemplation, in simplicity and the joy of charity — proclaims the presence of Jesus, instils enthusiasm in the young and multiplies vocations.

Joy and hope shine out among the fruits of the silence and the serenity flowing from the cross. From that ... Easter. From the mystery of Jesus, dead and risen again, is born the paschal newness of the consecrated life, a confirmation of the new life of Christ given through baptism (Rom 6:3-4). The paschal renewal of the religious — his genuine renewal in Christ through the Spirit — presupposes that he experiences deeply three realities: the meaning of the church, the depth of contemplation, and the joy of hope.

Every renewal in the consecrated life requires a profound living of the mystery of the church; the religious life has no meaning apart from its being within the

11

church: that must be perceived as a sacrament of the mystery of the risen Christ, a joyful mystery of fellowship, the sign and universal instrument of salvation.

A deeply contemplative inner life is also desirable. The church today must be more than ever the church of prophecy and of service; and that needs a permanent attitude of contemplation. Only persons capable of fruitful silence and serenity beneath the cross can truly be prophets and witnesses.

Finally, it is necessary to experience and proclaim the active joy of the christian hope. The religious life, a visible sign of the kingdom, must be a call to hope. Moreover, it must be a clear sign that hope is a firm call to trust in God, to fraternal fellowship and to creative zeal for the transformation of the world.

When St Paul invites us to "joy in hope", he does it in the paschal context of "sincere" charity. That is the meaning of the ecclesial community, the urgency of the new age and the clear invitation of the Spirit: "Rejoice in your hope, be patient in tribulation, be constant in prayer" (Rom 12:12).

May our Lady of Easter — the Virgin of the Cross, of hope, the Virgin of 'Let it be ...' and of the Magnificat — make us faithful messengers of deep joy and prophets of unshakable hope. This is my heartfelt prayer for all men and women religious throughout the world.

THE JOY OF PASCHAL RENEWAL

> We were buried therefore with him by baptism into death, so that as Christ was raised from the dead by the glory of the Father, we too might walk in newness of life (Rom 6:4).
>
> The disciples were glad when they saw the Lord (Jn 20:20).

Introduction

EASTER is a serene and profound call to joy. It is joy for the decisive victory of Christ over sin and death, joy for the world's reconciliation with the Father and for the unity of humankind, joy in the new creation coming from the Spirit. Prolonging the paschal mystery in our lives means making the joy of having seen the Lord clear to, and understood by, others. "I have seen the Lord" and also what he spoke of (Jn 20:18) "We have seen the Lord" (Jn 20:25).

The mark of a truly christian existence is joy. It is also the best testimony of authenticity in the consecrated life. It is not a matter of merely being individually cheerful, but rather, and above all, of forming paschal communities which live and irradiate joy daily. The best testimony of the primitive christian community — united in the word, the Eucharist and service — was "glad and generous hearts" (Acts 2:46).

Today we need to re-discover the joy of Easter. Indeed the worst sign of disorder in a community — christian or human — is sadness and fear. Jesus returns and asks us: "Why are you afraid? Have you no faith?" (Mt 4:40). Or: "Woman, why are you weeping?" (Jn 20:15). However, recovering the joy of Easter in the church and for the world means recovering the feeling of the cross. For

13

it is not a matter of superficial and ephemeral joy (which usually ends immediately), but of a deep and everlasting joy which comes only from the cross and is the fruit of "God's love ... poured into our hearts through the Holy Spirit who has been given to us" (Rom 5:5). "But the fruit of the Spirit is love, joy, peace ..." (Gal 5:22).

It is good for us to meditate on joy. Really, this means meditating on the essence of our Christianity: the Father's love, the cross of Christ, the fellowship of the Holy Spirit, the calm of prayer, the maternal presence of Mary. Speaking of joy does not mean ignoring pain, suffering and death. It means discovering the meaning of the cross as it comes from the fecundity of the paschal mystery.

St Paul describes the manner of life of an authentic christian community founded on love: "Be at peace among yourselves ... rejoice always, pray constantly" (1 Thess 5:12-20). The same bond between love and the cross, joy, hope and prayer is found in this magnificent exhortation to the Romans: "Let love be genuine ... rejoice in your hope, be patient in tribulation, be constant in prayer" (12:9-12). The paschal mystery is an inexhaustible source of true joy for us. It is the joy of being "a new creation" (Gal 6:15) and of living in the unshakable certainty of the near presence of the Risen Lord: "Rejoice in the Lord always; again I will say, Rejoice ... The Lord is at hand" (Phil 4:4-5).

I. The new-ness of Easter

Easter brings us face to face with the inevitable and joyful necessity of the new, the new in the world and in history, the new in ourselves and in the church. The presence of the risen Christ, the true "New Man" (Eph 2:15) is a firm call to us to deep renewal in the Spirit. "Cleanse out the old leaven that you may be a new lump, as you really are unleavened. For Christ, our paschal lamb has been sacrificed" (1 Cor 5:7). Easter

14

is the feast of Life, and therefore the celebration of the new. On the sacred night of the paschal vigil, the holiest, happiest and most profound night of the year, everything is new; light, water and bread; the bread of the Eucharist which makes us brethren, the water of baptism which makes us sons, the light of the risen Christ which makes us witnesses of his Passover.

But, above all, the one who is born again in Christ "of water and the Spirit" (Jn 3:5) is new. For this reason on the Easter Vigil — while we are singing the joy of the risen Christ and share in the maternal fecundity of the church which brings to birth new children in baptism — we renew our baptismal promises with greater feeling. If we have been buried with Christ in his death by means of baptism and identified with him in the resurrection, we cannot be persons old in sin (Rom 6:3-11), or those conquered by grief, pessimism or fear. We have been "born anew to a living hope through the resurrection of Jesus Christ from the dead" (1 Pet 1:3). At once people have the right to require of Christians "newness of life" (Rom 6:4), a new way of understanding and realising history, the paschal witness of a deeper joy and of a firmer and more creative hope, which are born from the cross of Jesus Christ and nothing else. Easter teaches us to read history from within and to value things and persons in accordance with their ultimate character. The individual is worth what the cross of Christ is worth. Because of it his life is sacred and his rights are inviolable. For "God so loved the world that he gave his only Son" (Jn 3:16).

This paschal invitation to renew ourselves — in our inner personality or in the life of our communities and institutions — is a call from providence to retain permanent youth; for that which frightens us is not death but old age. There is a way of getting old quickly — not being able to look at the world with new eyes every day, not being able to discern in our brethren a new aspect of Jesus every day, not being able to discover at every moment the daily new requirements of God's plan for us.

15

That is to say, it is a thinking that God's plan has been fully revealed to us once and for always, without allowing us the joy of continually uncovering an awe-inspiring and challenging surprise. There is a disturbing sign of our premature old age: it is allowing ourselves to be nostalgic about the past without doing anything to prepare for new things, with hope.

Contemplatives and the poor — those, that is, who live with a strong experience of God in the desert, or are permanently open to a deep communication of the word and to the joyful discovery of Christ in persons and in things — are the only people who are capable of savouring the joy of the new, and of understanding the true demands of the paschal newness. Those who live in the euphoria of what is purely external or in the improvisation of immediate changes, and those who shut themselves up in the private security of their own infallible judgement, are incapable of entering into the depths of the new, which continues to spring up every day by God's action in the world. For that reason too they are incapable of accepting generously the joyful responsibility of the new, and of experiencing it as a constant manifestation of God in history.

We need contemplatives, persons who see in history the presence of the risen Christ, who can announce to their brethren, as St John — the disciple whom Jesus loved, the contemplative — did: "It is the Lord" (Jn 21:7); persons who teach us not to be afraid in night or storm (Mk 4:35-41), but always to go forward without stopping to mourn over disasters or to lament our weariness; persons capable of anticipating in time the vision and certainty that eternal life has already been planted within us by baptism.

How lovely it is to think, with St Thomas, that "grace is the seed of glory"! How much we are encouraged by Jesus' words when he says that whoever believes in him and "eats his flesh and drinks his blood has eternal life" (Jn 6:47, 54). Let us walk now, in the nostalgia of exile

16

and the firm hope of pilgrimage, towards the final vision of perfect joy.

Genuinely to live the Easter life means experiencing the joy of a deeper meeting with Jesus the New Man, feeling the promise of profoundly renewing something in our life and those of others, and lovingly awaiting the final manifestation of Christ. Consequently the epitome of Easter newness is as follows: "If then you have been raised with Christ, seek the things that are above, where Christ is, seated at the right hand of God. Set your minds on things that are above, not on things that are on earth. For you have died and your life is hid with Christ in God. When Christ who is our life appears, then you also will appear with him in glory" (Col 3:1-4). Easter newness does not uproot us from history, it plunges us into it; it does not separate us from humankind, it opens us generously to our fellows. So far is it from shutting us up in time that it hurls us into the ultimate newness of eternity. For Easter makes us taste at the same time the joy of being "henceforward children of God" — and in consequence each individual's brother and sister — and the hope of being "like him for we shall see him as he is" (1 Jn 3:1-2).

II. The joy of living at this present time

The first thing asked of us Christians is that we love our own time, that we do not worry about what is happening nor dream superficially of a peace which does not stem from the cross. Christ re-established unity and brought peace to everything "by the blood of his cross" (Col 1:20). We must each of us discover the responsibility, the pain and the joy of our time, and the radical demands for renewal of the present. We must be faithful to Jesus Christ now; we must now live in the root meaning of the Gospel: the beatitudes and love, the desert and the cross, poverty and prayer, seeking the Father and serving the

17

brethren. What is it that the Lord asks of us today? What do my brethren hope and expect today?

There is a way of betraying our mission: it is by trying to escape from the present under the excuse that we are living in difficult times, full of insecurity and dangers. Anyone who is incapable of risking his own human security, has not yet learnt to be a Christian. "He who loses his own life, shall gain it". Certainly it is not a matter of squandering one's life in a superficial search for what is new, but of deriving from the paschal cross an inexhaustible source of deep and continuous renewal. "I make all things new" (Rev 21:5) is the clearest sign of the presence of the risen Christ. This makes us feel the joy and responsibility of facing the new age: as the one way of serving our brethren, and, above all of giving glory to the Father who loves us so much. Consequently, in the face of the challenge of the new age, one only answer remains: loyalty to our time, the irreplaceable joy of living in this, the only time that God has for us. "Now is my soul troubled. And what shall I say? Father, save me from this hour? No, for this purpose I have come to this hour" (Jn 12:27). But what do we mean by the new age? What is it like? Every life, if it be fully lived, is new every day. Individuals grow old at once when they resign themselves to accepting days as if they were irremediably and monotonously the same. If every day does not turn out to be new for us, we grow old in our work, in our personal relationship with those with whom we live, in our own christian existence, and in our priestly ministry or our consecrated life. Thus we get tired of things superficially repeated every day. We get used to living near a lake or a mountain. The sea causes us neither joy nor admiration. We even get used to people; so, frequently, it is easier to love a stranger or to be more encouraging or understanding towards those with whom we are not living. Without doubt, if love is real, it is constantly creative and, therefore, meets something new every day.

What is the new age like? We may look at it from

18

a simply human and immediate point of view, and so be either baffled and deflated, or we may be fired with enthusiasm and euphoria, and even with hope. It is simply the period in which we happen to live.

The first thing that occurs to us, from this simple human point of view, as we face this new age, is the pain of what is in front of us, which overwhelms us and which we do not understand. We do not understand, for example, why the world moves more and more towards violence and we see human beings becoming less humane, less fraternal and less sincere. One of the negative characteristics of today is mistrust; we are afraid of one another.

I turn to the new age of the church, that which starts, to specify a moment or an event, with the second Vatican Council. We constantly speak of a post-conciliar theology, a post-conciliar spirituality, a post-conciliar mentality, even of a post-conciliar church. This does not mean that the church before the council had been unfaithful to Jesus Christ. On the contrary; only with its creative productivity is it possible to understand the depth and spiritual richness of the church of today. However it is true that the Council did produce something new, just as something new ensued in Latin America after Medellin. How sad it would be not to be able to draw full profit from this powerful communication of the Spirit of God in both these saving events, and not to have taken in their profound demands. There are people in the church who thought we had a new church because of the introduction of certain changes which were rapid, surprising, without interior preparation, without a change of mind and heart, that is without a true conversion to God. The first requirement of paschal renewal is conversion. It is also the best path towards hope.

When the prophets proclaim the hope of future liberation, they always do so by means of the threat of punishment and a call to conversion. "Behold, the days are coming, says the Lord, when I will make a new covenant

19

with the house of Israel and the house of Judah ... . This is the covenant which I will make with the house of Israel after those days, says the Lord: I will put my law within them, and will write it upon their hearts; and I will be their God, and they shall be my people" (Jer 31:31-33). To the period of the dispersion and exile succeeded the new age of the return to the homeland and of national unity. This is conversion. We would like to live in the new age — of meeting, fellowship, unity and peace — without being converted.

There is a way of thinking of the new age as an age which we cannot escape living through, and so we suffer it sadly; we resign ourselves passively or we are worried. Yet there is another way of thinking of the new age — from a deeper and more prophetic point of view — as an age of unity and peace, fertility on earth and happiness in heaven, like the golden age, full no doubt of pain and suffering, but from which will arise justice, truth and love, in which "the wolf shall dwell with the lamb, the leopard shall lie down with the kid, and the calf and the young lion and the fatling together, and a little child shall lead them" (Is 11:6). It will be the new age of Jesus and the transforming presence of his kingdom. This age has already arrived and constitutes a call to repentance and faith: "The time is fulfilled and the kingdom of God is at hand; repent and believe in the gospel" (Mk 1:15). There are moments in history when the approach of Jesus and the demands for renewal made by his kingdom are in practice felt more strongly. Today we live in precisely one of these heaven-sent moments. Humanity's pain and the church's suffering proclaim to us that the paschal mystery has become more active in history and the call to inner renewal is stronger for the individual, for the christian community and for secular society.

There are new times which have overtaken us unaware, times which we ourselves bring about and unconsciously evoke because we are pleased by what is new and do not take account that it is something deeper and always requires a process of conversion and the joy of an Easter death. There are times which we desire and hope for and pray for but which never arrive. In the meantime we have to live with intensity and love this only hour that we have. We must neither be afraid nor allow it to pass without fully seizing it with the joy of faith.

The new age we are living through is, on the one hand, a time of superficiality and lack of confidence, of hate, violence and death, immorality, injustice and contempt of life. It seems to be "the hour and the power of darkness" (Lk 22:55). But, on the other hand, it is a time of contemplative inwardness, of seeking unity, of positive work for peace, of hunger and thirst for righteousness, of a clearer feeling of the presence of God, a greater consciousness of human rights and a greater participation by the young. It is an age which kindles our enthusiasm and cooperation, "Behold, now is the acceptable time; behold, now is the day of salvation" (2 Cor 6:2).

It is a joy to live now, in these difficult but God-given times of the kingdom, and to prepare strong and fruitful opportunities for the new generations, even if we must suffer much and die. We want times of prosperity and peace, of joy and hope, of true righteousness and brotherly love, times in which only the infectious joy of meeting, with the Father and the brethren, shines out, times in which we may experience God from within and may feel persons as friends. Then God's light will burst forth in our hearts like the dawn and we shall hear in the silence the Father's voice answering our cry: "Here I am!" (Is 58:9). In order to live in the new age with joy we must allow ourselves to be fundamentally converted by the Lord, and we must renew our baptismal pledge and the joy of being faithful to the covenant. "I will sprinkle clean water upon you, and you shall be clean ... a new heart will I give you ... and I will take out of your flesh the heart of stone and give you a heart of flesh. I will put my spirit within you" (Ezek 36:25-27).

III. Jesus Christ, the New Man, the Teacher of joy

It seems strange to think of the persecuted and crucified Jesus Christ, the austere Prophet of the inner life, of self-denial and the cross, as a teacher of joy. Certainly he was consecrated by the Spirit and sent by the Father to "preach good news to the poor ... and to proclaim release to the captives" (Lk 4:18). Jesus' message is the "glorious newness" of the kingdom; consequently, it is a constant invitation to the joy of repentance and faith, of prayer and the cross, of filial abandonment to the Father's care and of generous service to the brethren. In this too, Jesus is a "sign that is spoken against" (Lk 2:34). He teaches us that the source of joy is not success, till death. True joy is born from the depth of silence and from the fecundity of the cross. "If any man would come after me, let him deny himself and take up his cross daily and follow me" (Lk 9:23). "Unless a grain of wheat falls into the earth and dies, it remains alone; but if it dies, it bears much fruit" (Jn 12:24). Sadness is often born in us because we feel alone, or because we feel the barrenness of our work or the emptiness of our lives. Yet here is Jesus to fill it; here there is his paschal cross to give it fruitfulness and importance. To meet Jesus is to meet the true teacher of joy. His message is not of death but of life: "I came that they might have life, and have it abundantly" (Jn 10:10). Joy is the fruit of love which the Holy Spirit has poured into our hearts (Rom 5:5), and Jesus has come to show us the Father's love, to teach us to live in love and to bestow on us the gift of his Spirit. But for all this he wills the cross for us. "Greater love has no man than this, that a man lay down his life for his friends" (Jn 15:13). "Nevertheless I tell you the truth: it is to your advantage that I go away, for if I do not go away, the Counsellor will not come to you; but if I go, I will send him to you" (Jn 16:7). "In this the love of God was made manifest among us, that God sent his only Son into the world, so that we might live through him. In this is love, not that we loved God but that he loved us and sent his Son to be the expiation of our sins" (1 Jn 4:9-10). Revelation of the Father's love, experience of the Son's friendship through his death on the cross, bestowal of the gift of the Holy Spirit! This is the synthesis of Jesus' life and ministry. This is the source of our true joy.

Christ invites us from the beginning to be joyful. The sermon on the mount opens with the solemn proclamation of the joy of the poor, the meek, the mourners, of those who hunger and thirst for righteousness, the merciful, of those who are pure in heart, of the peacemakers, of those who are persecuted for righteousness' sake. All those are mysteriously and profoundly happy (Mt 5:3-12)! Therefore, a simple and complete loyalty to the Beatitudes would change the gloomy, aggressive faces of people. For this reason, above all, those who are consecrated — who have chosen of their own free will to be witnesses that the world cannot be transformed and offered to God except in the spirit of the Beatitudes (LG 31) — constitute for all, specially for the young, a clear testimony of the Father's goodness and a strong invitation to Easter joy.

Jesus' message centres in love (Mt 22:34-40), therefore its fruit is joy. It is joy in the Father's love (Jn 16:27), in trust in providence (Mt 6:25-34) and in the certainty of his forgiveness (Lk 15). It is the joy of remaining in the love of Christ by faithfully keeping his commandments: "These things have I spoken to you, that my joy may be in you, and that your joy may be full" (Jn 15:9-11). It is the joy of fraternal love, of generous service to the brethren and total self-giving to friends (Jn 15:12-13).

How much it costs us to be deeply and consistently joyful! The painful experience of our own personal sorrow, of our limitations and wretchedness, or of the suffering of our brethren, frequently hinders us from being serene, from being hopeful and spreading joy. Certainly in these critical and difficult moments, Jesus seeks us out and assures us of the perfect joy which is born from the cross.

23

"Truly, truly, I say to you, you will weep and lament, but the world will rejoice; you will be sorrowful, but your sorrow will turn into joy. ... But I will see you again and your hearts will rejoice, and no one will take your joy from you" (Jn 16:20-22). It is very significant that Jesus talks to us of joy when he is already living through the hour of his Passion.

Jesus plunges us into the source of joy, the mystery of his death and resurrection. It is the joy of the fruitfulness of his death, the salvation of humankind, the world's reconciliation with the Father, of fraternal fellowship, and of unity and peace. It is the joy of the love which made him obedient to the Father unto the death of the cross (Phil 2:8) and offer his own life for the redemption of his friends (Jn 15:13). The joy of the Incarnation reaches its fullness in Easter. It is the joy of Easter renewal. Jesus, the New Man, introduces us into the new life of God. We were far away, strangers to the community, without hope and without God in the world: "But now in Christ Jesus you who were once far off have been brought near in the love of Christ" (Eph 2:12-13).

It is important to understand Jesus making himself the New Man for us: the why and the how of it. For Jesus, with his cross, breaks down the wall of hostility between peoples and restores peace. It is worth while to quote the whole of St Paul's text for it is a very fine page of hope, inviting us to the joy of Easter renewal: "He is our peace, who has made us both one, and has broken down the dividing wall of hostility, by abolishing in his flesh the law of commandments and ordinances, that he might create in himself one new man in the place of the two, so making peace, and might reconcile us both to God in one body through the cross, thereby bringing the hostility to an end. And he came and preached peace to you who were far off and peace to those who were near; for through him we both have access in one Spirit to the Father" (Eph 2:14-18).

This is the outline of Easter renewal for the Christian:

life plunged deeply into the unity of the Father, the Son and the Holy Spirit, reconciliation, fellowship and peace. Division and selfishness, hatred and violence, injustice and death belong to the "old man". Easter renewal requires us to live in love, to practise righteousness, to be peacemakers. "If any one is in Christ, he is a new creation; the old has passed away, behold, the new has come. All this is from God, who through Christ reconciled us to himself and gave us the ministry of reconciliation" (2 Cor 5:17-18). From this arises St Paul's strong invitation to put off the old self — the self of sensuality, falsity and hatred — "to be renewed in the spirit of your minds, and put on the new nature, created after the likeness of God in true righteousness and holiness" (Eph 4:22-24; cf. Col 3:9-10).

This is ultimately the deep and infectious joy of the new self in Christ: the experience of the fatherhood of God, fraternal fellowship with all persons, sincerity and mutual trust, and positive work for the peace of the world.

What are the ways by which Jesus leads us to the new? Above all, revealing to us the secrets of the Father, inviting us to repentance and faith (Mk 1:15), and calling us to the true way of prayer and of the cross, of poverty and of love. The sermon on the mount is the best summary of the "new" in Christ. He does not come to destroy but to fulfil. The new in Christ is within us and complete. "Think not that I have come to abolish the law and the prophets; I have come not to abolish them but to fulfil them" (Mt 5:17). It is the indwelling and fullness of the Holy Spirit that Jesus was to send us from the Father as the fruit of his cross. When Jesus appeared, the Pharisees were shocked by the "new age": a great prophet cannot come from Nazareth, this is a carpenter's son, how can the Messiah die? how can he have seen Abraham? how can he rebuild the temple in three days? how can he forgive sins? why does he eat with sinners? They are questions which cannot be answered if we do not think of Jesus as the New Man who lives the disconcerting dimensions of the paschal mystery.

This New Man enters into the humanly inexplicable novelty of the Incarnation: "How can this be? ... The Holy Spirit will come upon you". Therefore, the Mystery of Mary "as moulded by the Holy Spirit and made a new creation" is "new" (LG 56). But the consummation of novelty in Christ is the foolishness of the cross. Only in the light of the paschal mystery of Jesus — death and resurrection — can we understand the fundamental novelty of Christ and what he came to bring us by the fellowship of his Spirit.

It is this Spirit who overwhelms us with joy. Christ has made us profoundly joyful. For this he has spoken to us of prayer and the cross; for this he bestowed on us the Spirit of love. Yes, Jesus is a teacher of what is within, not of superficial distraction. He is a serious but deeply joyful teacher. He had experience of sorrow and he sincerely wept. Yet he was not a sad teacher. Further, he does not allow us to be sad and to fast while the Bridegroom is with us. St Paul understood Jesus perfectly; that is why he talks to us so often of joy. For St Paul joy is connected with three things; the Lord's nearness: "Rejoice in the Lord always ... . The Lord is at hand" (Phil 4:4-5), the serene fruitfulness of the cross: "I rejoice in my sufferings for your sake" (Col 1:24) and the active presence of the Spirit: "You have received the word in much affliction, with joy inspired by the Holy Spirit" (1 Thess 1:6).

Jesus brings us the joy of the new. He is not merely a teacher of doctrine: he opens his side to us to give us "the water which gushes out into life eternal". Jesus unveils to us the way of the cross to reach the Father, to be his disciples, to be happy and fruitful. His message is always this: "Do not weep", "Do not be afraid", "Believe in God, believe also in me" (Jn 14:1), "The former things have passed away. ... I make all things new" (Rev 21:4-5). In the joy of paschal renewal, which is that of reconciliation and new life in Christ (2 Cor 5:17-18),

26

we are bound to meet the Father's love, the wisdom and strength of "Christ crucified" (1 Cor 1:23) and the transforming fellowship of the Holy Spirit. And we also meet, since it is a matter of the new life of the children of God, Mary, the "Cause of our joy". Through her came Jesus, the author of life, the Saviour of the world, the lord of history, the teacher of joy. In her — poor and contemplative, calm and strong at the foot of the cross, completely at the disposal of the Holy Spirit — we find the way to solid happiness in the realisation of the gospel beatitudes. By her and in her our sadness will be turned into joy, for in the hour of the cross — which will always be the hour of Easter — we shall find her near and on her feet. It will be the moment of privilege when we hear Christ repeating within us: "Behold, your Mother!" (Jn 19:27).

THE LORD'S DAY, A DAY OF MEETING TOGETHER AND SHINING FORTH IN THE RELIGIOUS LIFE

> Let the word of Christ dwell in you richly, as you teach and admonish one another in all wisdom, and as you sing psalms and hymns and spiritual songs with thankfulness in your hearts to God. And whatever you do, in word or deed, do everything in the name of the Lord Jesus, giving thanks to God the Father through him (Col 3:16-17).

> ... Be filled with the Spirit, addressing one another in psalms and hymns and spiritual songs, singing and making melody to the Lord with all your heart, always and for everything giving thanks in the name of our Lord Jesus Christ to God the Father (Eph 5:19-20).

Introduction

THE consecrated life — as a new and special deepening of the consecration of baptism — is a joyful celebration of the death and resurrection of Jesus; either it is lived as a special witness of Easter — with all that involves of serenity, of the cross and of joy in hope — or it does not make sense. Therefore, "joy" is an essential element in the consecrated life, as the fruit of a radical "following" of Jesus Christ, and a sign of his special presence in proclamation and anticipation of the final kingdom. "Rejoice in the Lord always ... the Lord is at hand" (Phil 4:4-5).

The first question we shall ask is this: Are we happy in the consecrated life? That is to say, do people notice in us the nearness of God and his kingdom, the procla-

28

mation of the Good News and the joy of salvation? Today's world — worried and divided but hungry for God — has need of the solid and close testimony of true paschal communities. People have a right to our joy. In the measure in which we live the "gospel beatitudes" to the very depth of our being we shall be truly happy and shall make others happy.

Now we ask ourselves what meaning has the "Lord's day" for us — for us who are consecrated. It is the same thing as to ask ourselves what meaning Jesus' Easter has for us. The first thing to ask ourselves is how we live on a Sunday, whether it is a full or empty day, joyful or nostalgic, boring or hopeful, of loneliness or fellowship, of inner contemplation or distraction, of apostolic glow or of egoistic absorption in the mere defence of our own salvation. How do we pass Sunday in our communities? How do christian people observe that we "celebrate" Sunday? Is it noticed that we have a paschal sense of deep, serene and infectious joy?

Speaking of the "Lord's day" — as a focal and splendid moment in the religious life — is speaking of the joy of Easter under these three aspects; the paschal character of the consecrated life, the inner life of contemplation and apostolic brightness.

I. The paschal character of the consecrated life

The consecrated life is a special conformation with the mystery of the death and resurrection of Jesus. It is a special proclamation of Easter, a mark, a testimony and a prophecy of the new life in Christ. Precisely as a special deepening of baptism, the consecrated life is also a deeper incorporation in the burial and resurrection of the Lord (Rom 6:3-4). For this reason it is a clear expression of the "new creation"; life according to the Spirit, liberty of the children of God, love of the brethren. Two passages from St Paul — fundamentally valid for every baptised

29

person — are particularly significant for the consecrated:

(a) "If then you have been raised with Christ, seek the things that are above, where Christ is, seated at the right hand of God. Set your mind on things that are above, not on things that are on earth. For you have died, and your life is hid with Christ in God. When Christ who is our life appears, then you also will appear with him in glory" (Col 3:1-4).

This is a text which is paschal and also eschatological. The religious, a pilgrim in time, is a symbol of eternal life which has already begun, a permanent challenge to seek for the good things which are invisible and to live in depth the true life of prayer, charity and the cross. The paschal mystery is essentially a mystery of love and hope. Such is also the consecrated life. Consequently, both are lived in a context of fruitfulness and festival.

The passage from Colossians just quoted ends with a series of practical exhortations which are summed up thus: "Do not lie to one another, seeing that you have put off the old nature with its practices and have put on the new nature, which is being renewed in knowledge after the image of its creator" (Col 3:9-10). It is the new man who lives essentially in charity (verse 14) and his characteristic is the peace to which we have all been called.

(b) "But whatever gain I had, I counted as loss for the sake of Christ. Indeed I count everything as loss because of the surpassing worth of knowing Christ Jesus my Lord. For his sake I have suffered the loss of all things, and count them as refuse, in order that I may gain Christ and be found in him, not having a righteousness of my own, based on law, but that which is through faith in Christ, the righteousness from God which depends on faith; that I may know him and the power of his resurrection, and may share his sufferings, becoming like him in his death, that if possible I may attain

30

the resurrection from the dead. Not that I have already obtained this or am already perfect; but I press on to make it my own, because Christ Jesus has made me his own. Brethren, I do not consider that I have made it my own; but one thing I do, forgetting what lies behind and straining forward to what lies ahead, I press on towards the goal for the prize of the upward call of God in Christ Jesus" (Phil 3:7-14).

This passage is also eminently paschal and eschatological. Paul has been conquered by Jesus Christ. He is now making his way towards the final meeting. He counts all things "loss" and "refuse" just to reach Christ, to "know him" in his deep experience of sufferings and death, of resurrection and life. Here again appears the theme of newness and the ultimate. Even if we live in time, we do not belong here below: our home is in the heavens; and "from there we await a Saviour, the Lord Jesus Christ, who will change our lowly body to be like his glorious body, by the power which enables him even to subject all things to himself" (Phil 3:20-21). The consecrated life is a continuous celebration of Easter. The very existence of the consecrated person is a permanent, explicit and concrete proclamation of the death and resurrection of the Lord. But this festal celebration has its peak moments in the consecrated life: the call and the response to it, first profession, perpetual vows, times of darkness and search, of special missionary detachment, of joyful acceptance of a providential but humanly inexplicable cross.

In this list the "Lord's day" also has its place: it is the day specially dedicated — in the light of Jesus' paschal mystery — to savouring in silence one's vocation, to pledging the joy of faithfulness, to reliving in depth the consecration made for ever within a settled community, to discerning together with others, in an atmosphere of prayer, the Lord's real requirements, to renewing the pledge

31

of closely following Jesus crucified and of giving oneself generously to the brethren. The "Lord's day" — weekly Easter of the consecrated life — is a high moment for inwardness and witness. We will talk of it later. But now I would like simply to emphasise three elements of the paschal nature of the consecrated life: sincerity of love, loyalty to the covenant and joy of hope. They are elements which define the consecrated life in its essence.

1. Sincerity of love

"Let love be genuine; hate what is evil, hold fast to what is good" (Rom 12:9). We are concerned with the joyful depth and of the completely unifying effect of love, made as an offering to the Father and a gift to men. Love explains, in its unbreakable unity, the paschal mystery of Jesus: obedience to the Father unto "death on the cross" (Phil 2:8-9), and giving himself to men for their ransom (Mt 20:28). There is need "that the world may know that I love the Father ..." (Jn 14:31). "Greater love has no man than this, that a man lay down his life for his friends" (Jn 15:13). The very same mystery lives in the consecrated life by virtue of the depth of the consecration to God expressed in the vows: a joyful and complete oblation to the Father and capability of service to the brethren. The two aspects cannot be separated — as it is not possible to separate two aspects of a similar commandment of love (Mt 22:36-40; 1 Jn 4:20) — but what gives the consecrated life its meaning is, above all, its relationship with God, its complete following of Jesus Christ. In the same way, what gives its true meaning to the paschal mystery is the explicit act of loving obedience to the will of the Father.

2. Loyalty to the covenant

The consecrated life reproduces the essence of the paschal mystery, the mystery of a covenant between God and creatures. It is a covenant of love, in which God holds the initiative [" ... Not that we loved God but that he loved us" (1 Jn 4:10)] and pledges his unbreakable faithfulness ["He who calls you is faithful, and he will do it" (1 Thess 5:24)]. The completion of a covenant which God has been attempting from the beginning, with Abraham, with Moses and the Prophets ("I will be your God and you shall be my people") is expressed in the paschal mystery. The unloosable tie of this covenant now passes through the heart of the cross ("This is the chalice of the new covenant in my blood"). The consecrated life actualises, sets forth and celebrates in a special way this inviolable covenant; further, it consists essentially in the unbreakable union between the love of God and the love of man. Consequently, it is exactly appropriate to place the consecrated life in this essential context of a covenant of love which best shows itself through demands which are sometimes hard and humanly inexplicable: depth of voluntary poverty, fruitfulness of celibate love, free self-annihilation of an obedience carried as far as the death on the cross.

The reality of the covenant — as much in the paschal mystery as in that of the consecrated life — makes us think of the joyful faithfulness of love, of the joy of fellowship and of the fecundity of reconciliation. For the consecrated life — like Christ's paschal mystery — is all this, a festal celebration of love, of fellowship, of reconciliation!, not only on the personal level but on that of the human race and universal history. It is from this that the consecrated life, fully lived, exercises an incalculable influence on society, even if it is the silent, hidden, unknown life of a contemplative monastery. Still further, only in eternity shall we be able to assess the fruitfulness in history — social and political — of a life lived in the austerity of contemplation.

3. *The joy of hope*

"Rejoice in your hope" (Rom 12:12). It is the normal fruit of Easter lived in the sincerity of love and loyalty

33

to the covenant and it is daily celebrated in the consecrated life. When this is lived in the sincerity of love it is a daily proclamation "of the good news" of salvation and an anticipation of what the supreme joy of the blessed will be in heaven. It is a calm and profound call to true joy: "Rejoice in the Lord always ... the Lord is at hand" (Phil 4:4-5). The fruit of the cross is always this: the joy of hope. "For in this hope we are saved" (Rom 8:24). "By his great mercy we have been born anew to a living hope through the resurrection of Jesus Christ from the dead" (1 Pet 1:3). The most tangible expression — for people's feelings — of an experience of God is joy. Consequently, people have a right to expect it of the consecrated. We are, by definition, "eye-witnesses" (Acts 2:32; 1 Jn 1:1) of Easter; and therefore, experts in joy and prophets of hope.

The Lord's day, in the consecrated life, must be a specially festive day, which shows forth the happiness of having been called, a deep, unspeakably infectious happiness which has its inexhaustible source in God only, and shows itself in us in the depth of our prayer, the serenity of our embracing the cross and the sincerity of our brotherly love.

II. Joy of the inner life

The Lord's day is a special moment for coming together in the consecrated life; it encourages us to the inner life of contemplation, to meeting in family, and to consciousness of a deep and firm incorporation in the church. The opposite of coming together would be isolation and dispersal, dullness and loneliness thought of as emptiness. The Lord's day, must, by definition, be the day of the joy of meeting with the Lord, with the community, with the church and with the whole of humanity. Coming together must occur on two levels, that of our own religious family and that of the local community of the people of God.

34

Let us speak, then, of inner family life and of incorporation in the church.

1. *Inner family life*

The Lord's day is a good opportunity — in a serene and joyful atmosphere — for enjoying the grace and responsibility of our own religious family, as the human family naturally does. It is thus a day for thinking over deeply, for being grateful for and for renewing, the promise of keeping faith with our own spiritual endowment. Above all, it is an opportunity for thinking again how this faithfulness may be of use in building up the local church: if it be in reality a faithfulness which is dynamic and ecclesial.

This inner family life — a true meeting with the Lord within the religious family itself — aims particularly at two things; so we are concerned to secure powerful moments of prayer (both individual and communal) and to make time for an authentic community life. Sunday in religious communities is often a sad, empty day: as if it were a day in parenthesis, when it should be the spiritual fount and fullness of the week. As a consequence the result may be a long and boring day. Each sister shuts herself up "on her own" to make up time lost during the week, to put her affairs in order, to bring her correspondence up to date or to prepare lessons. Little time is left for the family to meet, for reading, prayer and contemplation. Often enough, the only mark of Sunday, in some religious communities, is the almost private celebration of the Eucharist and the formal holding of a monthly day of recollection.

I would like to insist, from within the religious family, on these two requirements for the Lord's day: a greater depth of contemplation and a greater sense of fellowship in the community. For this reason, it is necessary to "respect" Sunday and to make full use of it.

When we speak of depth of contemplation we wish to insist on the possibility of a personal experience of

35

solitude, on the community's entering, "in poverty and simplicity", into the word of God, and on the celebration of calm and lengthy prayer. It is most important to make possible and to respect these great moments of prayer on the Lord's day. But let the prayer be a moment of tranquillity and rest — the rest suitable to contemplation — and let it always be made in an atmosphere of paschal serenity and festivity. Let the place be convenient for the meeting of the sisters; they are the beginning and end of the community's life.

The Lord's day — Easter, covenant, worship, assembly — is a special moment for living and celebrating the fellowship of the community, not only for resolving a problem but also for realising the Lord's presence: "where two or three are gathered together in my name" (Mt 18:20) and for thanking God for the gift of a real religious family. It is, therefore, the day of sincerity and discussion, of the exchange of experience of God and the church, of relaxation and meeting one another, and of fraternal correction and encouragement. Celebrating the community is not merely meeting together materially or expressing it in words. There must be the simple and fraternal acts of a community — presided over by the Lord and inspired by the Spirit — which lives by the word of God, the breaking of the bread and service to the brethren (Acts 2:42). There is something more: when we speak of "coming together" in the religious life we cannot think only of our local community: our religious family is more widely spread. There are, in particular, little isolated communities, living through difficult moments and in far distant missionary lands. We cannot celebrate the Lord's day in the true family spirit without having them, in their community difficulties and personal crises, in mind. The Lord's day is Easter for everybody.

Prayer and community! Two essential elements in the religious life; two aspects of the family inner life which it is fitting to rediscover and enter into more deeply every Sunday.

2. *Incorporation in the church*

All this richness of the religious life makes it necessary to live it within a local church. The Lord's day is, by definition, the day of the assembly, of the "ecclesia", of the people of God. This brings us to think of another essential aspect of coming together, that is of incorporation in the church. Every religious community exists within a parish or a diocese. It is absurd to celebrate Sunday outside any parochial or diocesan consideration. Therefore, except for due causes, it would be opportune on that day to take part in the liturgy of the assembly of the people of God gathered around the parish priest or the bishop. It would be a God-given moment for a personal meeting with the whole people of God, to celebrate together the same Easter of Jesus. It is not right to take part externally in the eucharistic assembly, without taking a personal interest in the problems of the others. It is the moment of a personal meeting — even if it be very silent and very short — with the priest or with the bishop, with all the members of the people of God, above all with the poorest and most needy. Ultimately, the religious life is a witness of the kingdom and an approach of God towards them.

Therefore the Lord's day — Christ's weekly Easter — must be, by definition, the church's day, not only out of consideration for the pastoral aspect of the religious life but also in the depth of that same life. The church needs my activity, but also my prayer. The church needs my work, but, above all she needs my silent loyalty to the gift of the Spirit.

For the consecrated life the Lord's day must be a pressing invitation to live the life of the church at all levels, beginning at the most immediate and ending in the true conception of the universal church. The word which the Pope pronounces every Sunday in Rome is a word which God pronounces to the church; and, therefore, he pronounces it to my community, he pronounces it to me. As for me, I must welcome it with joy, I must welcome it in poverty, I must carry it out loyally. It is also a word which my community will bring to life in silence for the whole church.

True integration in the church is bound to make us reflect on the problems of the world. The church is the "life and leaven of society" (GS 40), and the "universal sacrament of salvation" (LG 48). Therefore it is not possible to celebrate Sunday in the consecrated life without a special concern for the griefs and hopes of men. The consecrated life is a perpetual witness of Easter; but Easter is fellowship, reconciliation and peace. Sunday cannot be celebrated without a deep need for God and a real hunger for righteousness and love. Not every sister can betake herself to poor districts and make them feel the presence of Jesus there. But in the heart of every religious sister — sick, aged or contemplative — there will always be present Jesus living in the poor, the sick, and everyone who needs help (Mt 25:34 ff.).

III. Apostolic witness

In so far as the consecrated life truly celebrates Easter — that is, feels the joy of the paschal mystery which is brought to life in it and which it proclaims — it will be a genuine witness of the death and resurrection of the Lord. The Lord's day is a God-given opportunity for introspection in the religious life, from the personal, family and ecclesial point of view, that is, for taking cognizance of what it really means to be a religious, of one's obligations to the community and one's membership of a particular church.

It is from this that springs the joy of witnessing and the serene radiance of a life specially consecrated to celebrate the paschal mystery in its dual aspect (of the cross and of hope) and its two-way movement (of immolation to the Father and of bestowing salvation to men). If the consecrated life is lived fully in giving to the Lord (a radical "following" of Christ), every act and every duty is a manifestation of paschal joy, which the Holy Spirit brings to birth in the consecrated. The very existence of the religious — their presence in person and in community — is a tangible sign of the special presence of the Easter Christ. There is no time during the week when this clear demonstration, this shining Easter light and this communication of Jesus to others is not being given out. "Power came forth and healed them all" (Lk 6: 5-19). It is a special transmitting of calm and inner joy which can only come from a perfect harmony of love and is an evident sign and communication of Christ, "our blessed hope" (Tit 2: 13). There are, however, moments when this happens with particular spontaneity and providential effectiveness. Such, for example, is the Lord's day, since, as one is living with great intensity in the joy of consecration, the radiance of paschal rejoicing becomes more real. It is the joy of a Eucharist lived with special community fervour and it is feeling the joy of an assembly united by the Spirit, and the call to reproduce more deeply in one's own life the mystery of Jesus' death and resurrection, "that I may know him and the power of his resurrection" (Phil 3: 10). It is the natural radiance of the joy that springs from the experience of a true community (evangelical fellowship) and from finding again, every time more deeply and vividly, one's own spiritual endowment in the church.

For the consecrated life to become radiant there must be moments and periods of pure inner life in the Lord, privileged moments of prayer and community life. The paschal joy which shines out and is passed on must have its origin in the profound experience of God, in prayer and in the family meeting. But everything good is in its essence expansive. The joy of the experience of God in the consecrated life must be easily passed on to and received by others. The remainder of God's people, the whole human race, has a right to perceive the fruitfulness and joy of Easter as it is lived and experienced in the religious life.

The Lord's day is a day to be appreciated inwardly, but not a day of isolation or escapism. It is a moment of coming together to shine forth, and for shining forth in coming together. This comes out more easily if it is lived in a climate of strong churchmanship. There is no consecrated life which is not lived within a concrete church.

There are some aspects of this Easter radiance which I should like to emphasise. First of all comes the christian act (as in the gospel) of hospitality and genuine welcome. This requires communities which are open but very deeply-rooted. There is no question of losing or weakening the great moments of prayer and community life. The inner life of the community is always indispensable, specially on the Lord's day. But the prudent and wise inclusion of others in our personal experience of God may help them to share our family meeting more deeply and follow the Lord more thoroughly and exclusively.

In this same experience prayer meetings have their place. Today, more than ever, young people are coming to our convents and communities wanting prayer, and with a pressing need to learn to pray. Undoubtedly it would be a really evangelical response to their aspirations — and also a source of new vocations — if we were to set ourselves to pray simply with them, if we were to bring them effectively into our own prayer. Frequently the cry of the young generations comes to us: "Teach us to pray" (Lk 11:1).

Another way of spreading the paschal joy of the consecrated life is visiting the poor, the sick, the old and the needy of all kinds. It is a way of living the life of the gospel and putting the Beatitudes into real practice. But let them be normal, unfussy visits, springing from an inner abundance of charity, carried out in a cheerful atmosphere of Easter simplicity, and let them leave in the visited the taste and fruits of the Lord's passing by.

Finally, there is a way of spreading the joy of Easter on the Lord's day which is absolutely indispensable: it is the celebration of the feast by the community; let there be an atmosphere of Easter in the house (in prayer, in reading, in silence, in movement). It will only occur when there exist truly paschal communities, where the risen Christ is present and the transforming action of the Holy Spirit is felt almost sensibly; communities which are praying, fraternal, missionary, deep and open, characterised by simplicity and joy.

Radiance requires the witness of the whole community. When it is completely alive to, and passing on, the paschal presence of Christ, everybody feels affected, and vocations multiply. When the Lord's day is properly kept in a religious community — as a mark of a deep sharing in the Easter life of Jesus — everything becomes young and new.

Conclusion

For all this to be possible — for the Lord's day really to become a big moment of coming together and of radiance in the religious life — everything must be centred in the Eucharist. The Eucharist is the centre of the christian life and the source and fulfilment of the consecrated life. The latter is a daily celebration of the Eucharist, and therefore a continual celebration of Easter. In its turn, the celebration of the pascal mystery in the Eucharist — specially on the Lord's day — lights up and gives meaning and life to the consecrated life, pulls it together and offers it to the Father through Jesus Christ in the Holy Spirit.

In the eucharistic liturgy three parts are clearly distinguished: the Word, the Eucharist itself and the Communion. All that is confirmed in the consecrated life too. There is the mystery of the word which comes to us, enters our life and calls us: let us welcome it with

41

rejoicing and carry it out with a loyal response. This word is daily said to us anew, so our reply is equally new. Then comes the joyful immolation, the festive sacrifice, the deep transformation: thoroughly consecrated to the Lord, let us reproduce his image in a special way — conformed to his death and sharing in his cross and resurrection — "I have been crucified with Christ; it is no longer I who live, but Christ who lives in me" (Gal 2:20). Finally comes the communion: it is sharing, as a company of fellows, in the same body and in the same blood, it very strongly seals our unity and it commissions us to carry the fruits of the Eucharist — unity, love and peace — into the world.

This too is our consecrated life: after having experienced corporately the Passion of the Lord and the joy of the fraternal community, we go to meet the world, we enter into people's daily lives, we take a real share in their worries and experiences, we proclaim the Good News of Jesus explicitly to them, we deliver our peace to them, we call them to live in the joy of love and we invite them eagerly to await the coming of Jesus, who is our blessed hope.

May Mary accompany us with the strength of her contemplative silence and her loyalty. She lived the Lord's day deeply, as a consecrated person; in the plenitude of the cross and of hope, on the evening of the Friday and the morning of the Sunday. She lived it at Pentecost — the completion of Easter — in the inner life of the Spirit (prayer and fellowship having been made they " ... with one accord devoted themselves to prayer, together with the women and Mary the mother of Jesus, and with his brothers" Acts 1:14) and in the missionary radiance of the primitive church. She is today the image and principle of the church: virgin and mother. May she help us to live every Sunday and every day the mystery of the consecrated life, in the light of the mystery of Easter, with joy. May our consecrated life always be, like Mary and in Mary, a joyful immolation to the Father and a generous service to the brethren, a celebration of the fruitfulness of the cross and a witness and prophetic proclamation of hope. Thus there will be a daily celebration of the "Lord's day", while we wait, in the silence of the hidden life in the joy of giving, the glorious appearing of Jesus. Then will be the fullness of the "day of the Lord" for which we are all waiting, for it will be the final Easter.

THE JOY OF KEEPING FAITH

> Blessed is she who believed that
> there would be a fulfilment of what
> was spoken to her from the Lord
> (Lk 1:45).

ONCE again the subject of joy? And I think it is right, for there seems to be less of it about everywhere. So here is a new invitation to the joy of keeping faith, in the light of Mary, the faithful Virgin. It is the joy of a YES said wholeheartedly to the Father, and renewed every day in the consecrated life. It is the joy for a God who has put his mark upon us, who has set us as a seal upon his heart (Song 8:6), who has bound us with bands of love (Hos 11:4) and has sent us into the world to bear fruit which should abide (Jn 15:16). It is joy for a free choice, undeserved and mysterious, the choice of a God who calls us apart without cutting us off from our fellows, who nails us down firmly in the centre of the paschal cross and thence thrusts us out to spread the joyful news of Jesus to the brethren. "Rejoice ... for the Lord is at hand" (Phil 4:4-5). The consecrated life proclaims that the kingdom of God has arrived, the grace of God has appeared to bring salvation to all (Tit 2:11), and that Jesus is coming soon (Rev 22:20).

Joy is an essential element in the christian life; as love, of which joy is the first fruit, is essential (St Thomas 2, 2. 28). That fruit is particularly noticeable in *the consecrated life. A gloomy consecrated life is absurd and unthinkable: it would be an empty life, without the cross and the prophetic witness of Easter.* Yet this joy involves two things: unshakably believing that God loves us [("We know and believe the love that God has for us" (1 Jn 4:16)] and forcing ourselves generously to keep faith every day.

44

Being faithful to Christ, the church, and humankind.
Being faithful to our nature, to our specific quality of
consecrated people. Being completely ourselves in accordance with the adorable plan of the Father. Being immove-
ably faithful to the charism of our foundation. The Pope
constantly insists on this fidelity.

I. Fidelity to Christ, to the church and to humankind

We speak, first of all, of deep-rooted fidelity to Christ,
to the church and to humankind. *Basically, it is a single
and identical fidelity which is expressed simply by a radical
following of Christ who is alive today in the church with a
view to the complete salvation of humanity. The consecrated life is a sign of the absolute reality of God, a demonstration of his presence which requires two things: that the
symbol be immediately recognisable by persons and that
the central content of this sign be the belonging absolutely
to God, who must be loved above everything.*
If we had to define this fidelity to Christ more precisely, we should be bound to say that it is necessary
joyfully to enter into the totality of his message, to be
poor, to receive his word in silence and to embody it as
did Mary. That is the secret of happiness, as Jesus affirmed
(Lk 11:27). Fidelity to Christ involves a particular conformity to his death and resurrection. The consecrated life
reproduces in a special way the picture of Jesus praying
and crucified, worshipping the Father and serving men.
*Being faithful to Jesus is having the ear alert for his abso-
lute and daily renewed demands.* One cannot modify the
offering made to the Lord, nor think of having made it
just once and for always. The definitive offering once made
— e.g., on the occasion of perpetual vows — requires a
determined loyalty and a new beginning every day: yes,
today the Lord asks something new of me, for every day
there is something new happening in the story of salvation
and thence there is something new that I must joyfully offer.

Being loyal to Jesus is living permanently in a contemplative frame of mind, calmly producing the fruits of the cross and gladly giving help to the brethren. Being loyal to Jesus Christ is living the consecrated life in its essence thoroughly, without losing time over superficial external arrangements. In short, it is allowing oneself to be deeply penetrated by the gospel and to be led exclusively by the Spirit. The consecrated life, as a deepening of baptism, is really life *in accord with the Spirit*.

Yet this loyalty to Christ must always be practised within the church, which is essentially the presence and communication of the paschal Christ: "Christ in you, the hope of glory" (Col 1:27). Loyalty to Jesus Christ is inseparable from complete loyalty to the church in its total mystery: as sacrament of Jesus Christ, the church is, in its turn, a community of faith, hope and charity, indwelt by the Holy Spirit, and visibly built up by the hierarchy and the sacraments. The church is indivisibly spiritual gift and institution.

Being faithful to the church is, therefore, being faithful to the demands of the Lord, who is its head, and of the Holy Spirit who dwells in it. Loyalty to the church requires us to go beyond human limits and penetrate by faith into the heart of its mystery. Yet the church is a fellowship with the Trinity, living in time; it is a constant recall to renewal in the Spirit and to a deep repentance, in order to respond adequately to the needs and expectations of the people of today. There is no loyalty to the church without a deep conversion to Jesus Christ. However, an authentic conversion to Christ implies a continual look towards the human person with a view to his salvation. It implies also a joyful and complete fellowship with the Pastors.

Being loyal to the church is loving it with its human limitations, as we accept, love and are grateful for the human limitations of Jesus Christ (his weakness, poverty, incarnation and death on the cross). If we do not love the church as she is — even in the poverty of her Pastors and the sin of her members — we have not understood the mystery of the Incarnation, nor the wisdom and power of the cross. This causes us to exercise our loyalty in any demands which the church may make upon us, demands which humanly speaking upset us, or may seem hard and incomprehensible to us. Here too we must be *consistent.* There exist in the church clear rules about its *Magisterium,* which cannot be ignored or disobeyed, much less argued about or rejected. Instead they must be accepted in faith, in the light of the cross and of Easter.

Loyalty to Christ and his church implies also loyalty to the people of today, bearing in mind their legitimate expectations, but always looking at them from our position as religious.

The incorporation of religious in the world which the church brings about — a historical implication of their existence as consecrated persons — must be effected always bearing in mind their particular origin. The spheres of laity, consecrated laity, and religious — each valid in its ecclesial and evangelical sense — are not to be confused. The world, man, and history appeal to us, but in different ways. The missionary obligation, too, is valid for everyone, but is fulfilled in different ways. Otherwise the church would be put into the position of being a fellowship (variety in harmony with the Spirit) with the end of turning itself into a uniformity. To each of us the Spirit allots his gifts in a different way for the common good (1 Cor 12).

Keeping faith with the people of today means taking on their worries, hopes, griefs and joys (GS 1); it means sharing their loneliness and poverty, the which demands of consecrated souls a great capacity for contemplation and an inexhaustible urge for serving. Keeping faith with people also means — and this is fundamental — another thing, which is knowing how to arouse in them the hunger for the absolute, for God, to give to them every day the peace, the joy and the hope which are born of the Holy Spirit (Rom 15:13), to introduce to them the enjoyment of fellowship with God and the brethren, and to help them to walk together in the path of hope till they reach final happiness. Keeping faith with people is not merely teaching them patiently to hope for their future fatherland, and not even making them keen to live in the illusion of incomplete happiness or an initial and temporary liberation. The consecrated life — if it is a truly faithful witness of Easter and truly prophetic — will be a visible sign of God and a real communication of his presence. Therefore, keeping faith with people means making their complete salvation and their full liberation in Christ possible, awakening in them the hunger for truth and the good, and satisfying their deepest longings for the peace and hope to which we have been called.

II. What the church expects from the consecrated life

This fact makes us think of another thing. Men and women religious frequently ask us: What does the church expect of the consecrated life? The reply would take too long. For first we should have to answer another question, which is: What is the church? The church is Christ in our midst. Then the original question becomes this: What does Christ expect of us in the consecrated life, today? Further, the church is all the people of God (bishops, priests, religious and laity). The question then would be: What do these — all these, in accordance with their points of view and their different positions in the church — expect of the consecrated life? An institute cannot, however important it be, organise its own scheme of life independent of the ecclesial community, presided over by Peter and the Apostles, that is by the Pope and the bishops. In preparing and putting into practice such a scheme, the judgement of the Spirit calls for a special effort of fellowship. It is to be a way of living — often passing through the darkness of faith — in the joy of loyalty. The question "What does the church expect from the consecrated life?" can then be translated thus: "What do the priests and laity expect of our activity and manner of life, our presence and mission, our behaviour and practical works?" But, above all, what do the Pope and bishops expect? — inasmuch as it is on them, ultimately, that the Lord has built the church which is indefectibly indwelt by the Holy Spirit.

Taking a serious view of the consecrated life — above all of certain attitudes and concrete activities — there is no doubt that many things would change if we were to answer faithfully this question: What do Christ, the ecclesial community and the world expect of us? Anyhow there are three aspects of the consecrated life which it is useful to emphasise: the church expects of religious that they should be faithful to their original nature, to their essential nature and to their present nature.

Being faithful to their *original nature* means living fully, faithfully and gladly in their special position in the church. Religious are, first of all, Christians, but Christians in a way undoubtedly different from others. This very difference, when it is taken to be a special and joyful *following of Christ*, becomes a special way of prophesying; it becomes an explicit proclamation of the kingdom, a denunciation of every sort of sin, and an urgent call to repentance. Their *origin* does not put religious at a distance from other members of the people of God, nor does it separate them from the world: on the contrary, it *distinguishes* them and fits them into their own unmistakable *special place*. It makes them live and feel with the people, in a deep human and christian solidarity, endowing them, however, with a wealth of their own, a special gift, which marks them out and makes them profitable for others.

The loss of the original nature of the consecrated life is today one of the causes of the lessening of vocations. Whenever identity disappears or becomes a matter of controversy, it is natural for young people to lose enthusiasm and direction. Keeping faith with originality is then assuming a great urgency with God and with men and this at

D

rock bottom belongs to the essence of our vocation, our consecration and our mission. We are happy in proportion to our complete loyalty to our consecration, that is to our specific identity as men and women who have received a very special call, been mysteriously changed and are constantly sent into the world as witnesses of the kingdom who are easily and clearly recognisable.

Another aspect which it is worth while to emphasise, and is what the church expects of religious, is fidelity to the essential values of the consecrated life. What does this *essentiality* in the religious life mean? It means that we must not get lost in unimportant matters. What is really important is our complete self-giving to Christ in poverty, chastity and obedience. The essential lies just here: that the consecrated life be truly thought of and treated as a joyful response of love to a God who first loved us. The religious life reproduces in a privileged manner the mystery of Easter: death and resurrection, cross and hope. In this way it is inscribed at the heart of the covenant. God who is utterly trustworthy makes a covenant with his people. The religious life is a sign of God's trustworthiness when, that is to say, it is lived in the deep and serene joy of love. Persons must easily perceive in us and in our manner of life the fact that God has visited and redeemed his people (Lk 1:68). The religious life must be a clear sign that God is at hand, a manifestation of his love and a permanent invitation to joy.

Being faithful to the essential in the consecrated life is opting decisively for Jesus Christ who has made us his own (Phil 3:12). How lovely it is to feel bound to Jesus by the Spirit! It is the true liberty of the evangelical counsels; the vows do not destroy personality; rather, they are the perfect realisation of our free and complete capacity for loving. They must therefore be fulfilled in their essential character as a glorious sacrifice to the Father, through Jesus Christ, in the Holy Spirit.

It is, to sum up, a matter of living fundamentally as St Paul says: "Whatever gain I had, I counted as loss for the sake of Christ. Indeed I count everything as loss because of the surpassing worth of knowing Christ Jesus my Lord. For his sake I have suffered the loss of all things, and count them as refuse, in order that I may gain Christ and be found in him ... that I may know him and the power of his resurrection, and may share his sufferings, being like him in his death, that if possible I may attain the resurrection from the dead" (Phil 3:7-10).

Knowing Christ is sharing his humiliation and his exaltation, his absolute conformity to the Father and his fruitful gifts to the entire human race. It is having experience of the love of God. Being faithful to the essential in the consecrated life is living to the full in the joy of poverty, chastity and obedience, which means that we are bound to live in a constant atmosphere of faith, hope and charity. It is only from this fully theological character that the vows acquire luminosity, strength and richness.

I must also emphasise strongly other essential values with which the young of today are particularly concerned. They are prayer, the community and missionary energy. Without these values no authentic Christianity and, much more, no religious life exist. We have, therefore, to form new paschal communities where there is experience of the risen Christ and of the transforming activity of the Holy Spirit; communities which are fundamentally contemplative, fraternal and missionary.

If one wishes to make a valid appraisal of the authenticity of the consecrated life, one ought to enquire whether there exists in it a genuine hunger for prayer, the joy of evangelical brotherhood and a lively missionary sense. Today a sign which is most positive and promising for the future of the consecrated life is the desire for prayer — personal and corporate, liturgical and spontaneous — based on the word of God, sincere and concerned with the disquiet and hope of humankind; it is a true sign that the consecrated life aims at being a powerful experience of God, as an evangelical response for the transformation of the world.

A third aspect of happiness in the consecrated life is its *present nature*. This does not mean an easy and superficial adaptation to the new age, but a way in which God affects us deeply through the events of history. We must read the signs of the times with the key of faith; and therefore we cannot fail to be contemplative. Today we have to be very attentive to the demands of the Spirit and to let ourselves be led by him. Being up to date makes us accept the providential challenge of our time, that we love it gratefully and live it with calm intentness. Being up to date does not mean a dangerous and unacceptable involvement with the world but an ever deeper return to Jesus Christ and the totality of his gospel. The social changes, rapid, deep and universal as they are, cannot modify the essential values of the consecrated life; but they must make them clearer and more noticeable. Being brought up to date does not mean being modern and accepting any suggestion whatever, but being more authentically evangelical.

Keeping faith with the present day, then, requires two things of us; discovering with gratitude and trust and the key of faith, the measure of the Lord's road through history, and living on his terms (with his support) in the joy of conversion. Let us not be afraid of difficult times, but let us meet them generously in hope. When we speak of the present nature (brought up to date) of the consecrated life, we mean the process of a profound renewal in Christ, a desire for greater silence and prayer, a greater love of the cross, and a total and more missionary sort of giving in the service of our brothers and sisters.

In conclusion we will say: we are to be more obvious signs of the holiness of God, witnesses of the kingdom, prophets of Easter, and that means returning to the essence of our fidelity to consecration, which carries us to the inexhaustible source of a joy which is very deep and stimulating, imperturbable and serene, which is born of the cross of Christ and brings us the renewing power of the Spirit.

III. The faithfulness of Mary

At the moment of the Annunciation, the angel summoned Mary to joy: "Be of good cheer, O full of grace, the Lord is with thee" (Lk 1:28). Elizabeth proclaimed her "blessed" for having believed, for having proffered that YES, for having remained faithful. And the Virgin in her turn was to sing the joy of God's faithfulness to his promises (Lk 1:44-45). The faithfulness of Mary has its being in detachment and poverty, in contemplation and the cross, in readiness and trust. Mary begins by believing in God's faithfulness: hers depends on him to whom "nothing is impossible" (Lk 1:37), on him who "has regarded the low estate of his handmaiden" (Lk 1:48). Mary's faithfulness too meets moments of sadness and difficulty. For example, she has difficulty in understanding the reply which her Son makes to her in the temple (Lk 2:50) and suffers deeply in herself the martyrdom which Jesus suffers on the cross (Jn 19:25). Hers is a faithfulness which grows in understanding and fruitfulness, and is worked out in serene and joyous silence.

In the light of the Madonna we understand three things: faithfulness consists in always saying "Yes" to the Lord; one must be faithful to the Father in silence and on the cross; and fidelity is made up of poverty, trust and readiness to respond. It is only the poor who can cherish full trust in the Lord, depend upon the ineffable certainty of his love, and pronounce their "Yes" from the heart.

We offer ourselves to God because we trust him. The fears and limitations of our human loyalty are shown up by the infinite and unceasing loyalty of God. We have given ourselves to a God who is never less than his promises and who is with us always.

There are moments of crisis which test the loyalty of consecrated persons, sad moments full of uncertainty and questioning, of pessimism and weariness, of disappointment and dejection. In these moments, alas, even splendid vocations can fail ... when the world was expecting much of these consecrated lives, from their glorious fidelity to the specific and essential quality of the life of consecration, and when, above all Christ had placed so much faith in them, projecting them to transform the world with the spirit of the beatitudes.

However, even in view of these happenings we need not allow ourselves to be overcome by sadness and lack of confidence. Indeed it is just the moment when we must renew "the joy of hope" (Rom 12:22), and base on Christ, "the faithful witness" (Rev 1:5), the joyful fruition of our "Yes" to the Father. Let the difficulties of the moment we are living through, or the consciousness of our personal limitations, or those of the institute to which we belong, never interfere with the strength of the bond of our loyalty, nor lessen the joy of our self-giving.

Living "the joy of our faithfulness" is having the certainty that God loved us first, has chosen and consecrated us in the Spirit, and sends us daily into the world as signs of his presence and witnesses of his kingdom. We are sure that there was a moment when the Lord mysteriously entered our lives and called us. Like Samuel we too replied: "Speak, for thy servant hears" (1 Sam 3:10), or indeed like Mary: "Behold, I am the handmaid of the Lord; let it be to me according to your word" (Lk 1:38). In that moment we felt an ineffable joy, the fruit of our first sincere and clear response. Then we embarked on a serious course. Perhaps, immediately afterwards, we met difficulties, times changed and we began to doubt ... . In these moments of darkness and tension it became clear to us how very providential is the word of God: "Do not be afraid, I am with you".

The world expects a paschal witness from our lives as consecrated persons, that we really be prophets of a living God. So, it is necessary to live in depth the joy of our fidelity to our vocation, to our consecration and to our mission. "Rejoice always, pray continually (1 Thess 5:16-17).

Poverty and hope, contemplation and the cross, fidelity and joy: of these values the world has need. This is what Christ requires of us. The consecrated life, lived in the paschal quality of the covenant and as a sign of the continual presence of the Lord of the world's peace, will be an evangelical response to the sadness and worry of the world of today and the most attractive invitation to the joy of salvation.

It is the prophetic proclamation — expressed in words and deeds, by people and communities — that the kingdom of God has arrived and that Jesus lives with us to the end of the age (Mt 28:20). This will teach us to live as Mary, the faithful Virgin and the cause of our joy. By means of her and in her we shall be faithful. Drawing upon her, we shall teach the world to be faithful.

THE TESTIMONY OF THE LIFE
EXPECTED OF RELIGIOUS

> The life was made manifest, and we saw it, and testify to it (1 Jn 1:2).
>
> You shall be my witnesses in Jerusalem and in all Judea and Samaria and to the end of the earth (Acts 1:8).
>
> You are a letter from Christ delivered by us, written not with ink but with the Spirit of the living God, not on tablets of stone but on tablets of human hearts (2 Cor 3:3).

Introduction

BEARING witness to the Life, to the Life which is Christ, to the eternal Life which we bear, proclaim and await, is the mystery of the consecrated life, firmly incorporated in baptismal consecration and specially distinguished by the cross and by the hope of Jesus' paschal mystery. Here we touch the essence of the consecrated life, as being a clear sign, noticed at once, of the presence of a God who is love, and a letter of Christ easily "known and read by all men" (2 Cor 3:2). This requires a continual effort to be sincere and simple. The world of today is particularly sensitive to the essential values of the religious life.

We speak immediately of the "testimony of life", and thus we are discussing the *very being* of the religious life, and not merely of pastoral work or apostolic activity, even if these also — as manifestations of a life and the fruit of the Spirit's action — can give a testimony which is easily recognisable by the world. "The works which the Father has granted me to accomplish, these very works which I am doing, bear me witness that the Father has sent me" (Jn 5:36).

Our business now is to discover the *manner of life* which can most easily reveal to the people of today the true likeness of God and the coming of his kingdom, and may, at the same time, be the manifestation of the saving presence of Jesus and a continual invitation to repentance.

The consecrated life must essentially be a revelation of the love of God, a concrete sign of the covenant and an irresistible invitation to fellowship between individuals themselves and with God. Therefore, it must be lived in "genuine love" and "rejoicing in hope" (Rom 12:9-12).

I would like to draw attention to three points which impress me as fundamental for the witness of life which is expected of us today — poverty, prayer and evangelical brotherhood. I should like these simple reflections, which are already well-known, to be a sort of examination of conscience, made in the light of God's word and the growing expectation of today's world, an examination which faces us with the irresistible and joyful necessity of "being renewed" by the deep and infectious novelty of Easter: "If you have been raised with Christ, seek the things that are above, where Christ is, seated at the right hand of God. Set your minds on things that are above, not on things that are on earth. For you have died, and your life is hid with Christ in God. When Christ who is our life appears, then you also will appear with him in glory" (Col 3:1-4). That is a magnificent Easter text, which expresses the responsibility and the fundamental lines — death and resurrection, detachment and an inner life of contemplation, presence in history and eschatological tension — of a new life in Christ. Ultimately, indeed, the consecrated life is a sign and anticipation of "the new nature, created after the likeness of God in true righteousness and holiness" (Eph 4:24). A sermon or an article on the novelty of Easter is perhaps understood only by initiates; but the evidence of a really new life in Christ is easily understood by the poor and simple. It would be well to remember them more often, not to be sorry for them nor to evangelise them, but rather to experience the joy of being evangelised by them.

I. Poverty

"Blessed are the poor in spirit, for theirs is the kingdom of heaven" (Mt 5:5).

Speaking of poverty daunts me, simply because I am not poor. I know indeed that poverty requires a radical detachment from oneself, a serene self-abandonment as far as to the death of the cross and a permanent readiness to welcome, listen to and serve the brethren. Fortunately, poverty is also a total abandonment in the hands of God, and that gives me confidence.

Yet speaking of poverty also daunts me because, when one sets out to say much about poverty, a new way of being rich appears. He who is really poor never clearly takes note of it. He loves poverty and tries to enjoy it in silence, but fears that he may lose it if he shows it, and much more, when he rigorously demands it of others. Therefore, he simply lives in it.

If there were greater poverty among us, there would be fewer divisions. Indeed we should be less concerned about our own personal security and more ready for dialogue with our brethren. Furthermore, we should learn truly to pray together and to wait upon the Lord for everything. Many communities find themselves disintegrating for lack of poverty, because one way and another, they feel the immovable belief that they are faithful to their charism and have a monopoly of perfect loyalty to the church. Poverty makes us fundamentally insecure and dissatisfied with ourselves: but it is a temporary insecurity and a serene dissatisfaction, which is at once ready for prayer, for genuine concern for others and for filial self-abandonment in the hands of a Father who is omnipotent and never fails us.

For this reason, poverty is never aggressive, violent and exclusive: it is essentially serene and cheerful, shows itself in a strong capacity for universal love (from which no one is excluded) and seeks with simplicity to reach all human beings to tell them — with the cry of silence and the witness of being there — that the kingdom of God has arrived and that one must repent and believe the Good News (Mt 1:15). Poverty is thus a proclamation of the kingdom of justice, love and peace, and it is a prophetic denunciation of attitudes and patterns which obstruct the perfect sharing of its fruits.

When he says to us: "Blessed are the poor in spirit" Jesus does not mean to reduce poverty to no more than an inner attitude, but to indicate to us the spirit with which exterior conduct must be treated: selling everything and giving the price to the poor and following him (Mt 19:21) or even: "the Son of man has nowhere to lay his head" (Mt 8:20).

The Lord asks us a true and effective poverty, detachment from every human form of security (ability, money, material goods, temporal powers), and a real witness of simplicity and evangelical freedom. He also asks of us, as a pledge of his presence and mission, a special love for those who lack everything: house, bread, work, health, love, hope, joy and experience of God's fatherhood. In a way it is that kind of poverty described by St Paul: "You were at that time separated from Christ, alienated from the commonwealth of Israel, and strangers to the covenants of promise, having no hope and without God in the world" (Eph 2:12).

We have been chosen and consecrated by the Spirit to bring the Good News to the poor. But who are the poor? Without entering into a deep biblical, theological and social enquiry I would say that "a poor man" is anyone who lacks the elementary necessities of life, he who lacks bread on the family dinner-table, he who lacks food, clothing, health and work, the meaning of life and the company of friends, culture and a real sharing in carrying

59

out his own vocation and the history of his people, love, joy and hope, the word of God, faith and the life of Christ in the Eucharist, he who lacks experience of God the Father, and the neighbourliness of his fellows as brothers, he who feels himself to be inevitably alone.

Today we are required to have a special solidarity with the poor, to share the experience of their pain, their loneliness and their expectations, not so as to remain in their condition for ever, but to give them a sense arising out of faith and to help them to overcome everything in charity. "Christ, though he was rich, yet for your sake he became poor, so that by his poverty you might become rich" (2 Cor 8:9). Poverty is not an end in itself, but a way of living in the charity which "hopes all things, endures all things" (1 Cor 13:7).

When we speak of a poorer manner of life, we think of a special call of the Lord to live in simplicity, both as individuals and as a community, to find out and share closely in the lack of human security, the pain and the expectations of the poor. It is the sense of real closeness to the poor, of opening our houses to them, and of the establishment of a true evangelical brotherliness (always realised within the ecclesial community and in accordance with our own charism) in the midst of the most needy of people. As a general rule, almost all the institutes came into being as an evangelical response to extreme moral, spiritual and material poverty in particular urban and rural surroundings. We only have to consider whether our manner of life really responds to the wish and grace of the founders.

I should like, however, to add some further considerations. When we talk of "choosing the poor" from the point of view of the consecrated life, we mean a deep-rooted choice of "Jesus Christ, the poor man". What gives meaning to our consecration is its special relationship with Jesus Christ; otherwise our choice would be purely sociological and not even exclusively christian (starting from another ideology, it would be possible to make the same choice with a contrary intention). It is therefore important to adopt generously and joyfully the total detachment of Christ who "though he was in the form of God, did not think equality with God a thing to be grasped, but emptied himself, taking the form of a servant ... and being found in human form he humbled himself and became obedient unto death, even death on a cross" (Phil 2: 5-11). True poverty in the consecrated life is always a part of the mystery of the kenosis of Jesus.

Our choice of the poor, then, is truly integral (the whole person), universal (everyone) and saving (specifically christian and evangelical). A choice of the poor is always calm, joyful and universally fraternal. It arises from a deep vision of faith and an irresistible experience of the love of Jesus Christ present in humankind: "I was hungry and you gave me food, thirsty and you gave me drink, I was a stranger and you welcomed me, I was naked and you clothed me, I was sick and you visited me, I was in prison and you came to me" (Mt 25: 34-36).

A true choice of the poor does not exclude — it rather requires — a deeply evangelical work with other social classes who live in plenty and who need to be brought up in the faith, trained in a real sense of justice and urged to live in continued efforts of christian charity. Here is the drama of many people and communities who feel called to live among the poor and choose the poor. How are they to do it? There are two ways equally christian and evangelical, even if on differing levels of depth and effectiveness. One is the obvious one: to take up permanent residence in a poor and needy district and to give there a witness of the poor Christ by sharing the lot of the others. The other is slower and more hidden: to remain there to train christian communities (of the young and of adults) keen on their faith and evangelically aware of the great needs of the poor. Sometimes, this way is more painful, apparently useless and criticised, but, in the long run, if it takes up the cross of Christ in the gospel sense, it is much deeper and more effective, because it multiplies the true evangelisers of the poor. Such is the case of Catholic colleges — when they are real centres of evangelisation — and of other educational and relief works.

Finally, a last reflection on our choosing of the poor. It must start from an essentially evangelical consideration and from our special responsibility as being consecrated people. In other words, it must always be a presence of Jesus with a view to salvation, a clear proclamation of his kingdom of truth, holiness and grace and a firm invitation to hope. There is one thing which the poor have a right to expect of the consecrated: the specific proclamation — in words and community acts — of the joyful News of the coming of Jesus, the Saviour. They need to see us very close to them in their sufferings, even though they understand that we cannot provide a solution to all their problems. They do not want to feel that we are like those who confine themselves to "sympathising" with their poverty, but like those who are able to "take it on" in their love so as to redeem themselves in it. They want us to feel happy at sharing the poverty of others, to feel happy at giving them a sense of hope like an open door to the kingdom, to feel extraordinarily happy at being poor in this way, so poor that we can only offer them the fruits of our own cross, the nothingness of our consecration, the sincerity of our love, the joy of our hope and the infallible effectiveness of the apostolic words: "I have no silver and gold, but I give you what I have; in the name of Jesus Christ of Nazareth, walk" (Acts 3:6).

II. Prayer

"Lord, teach us to pray" (Lk 11:1).

"Rejoice always, pray constantly" (1 Thess 5:16-17).

The world of today — specially that of the young — needs to pray and thirsts to pray. Therefore we are bound to be not only "men of prayer" but also "teachers of prayer". Why is there this demand for prayer from people who have known technology and science and the seductive temptation of politics at first hand?

It is a fact that — at least in some countries — contemplative monasteries are besieged by men and women who feel an urgent need to experience God deeply and to listen to him. Is this simply disenchantment with life or an avoidance of work for others? In the majority of cases it is not: it is rather a search for reality and depth, and for true fellowship with God and with man, things which make people feel a longing for silence, a need for prayer and a taste for contemplation.

Religious communities, most of them, are finding their renewal in a deeper desire for prayer, a desire which is felt most deeply by the younger men and women religious. I would dare to say that this is the most visible positive aspect of present day renewal. Unfortunately — we must sincerely recognise this too — it does not always happen thus. There are cases where the insufficiently thought-out pursuit of new forms of prayer has resulted in the suppression or neglect of those that are traditional and the consequence has been a fall into emptiness. There are also cases where the lure of apostolic activity, of professional work or of political effort has resulted in the abandonment of every type of prayer.

Yet this is not the phenomenon which is most characteristic of the majority of religious institutes. There is a clear and joyful manifestation of the Spirit's calling to inwardness and silence, to the desert and to fellowship, to hearing the word of the Lord and to celebrate it in the Eucharist. The first thing to be noted in this prayer is its genuine hunger for the word of God. Once we sought other books and recited set forms; now we appreciate God's word more deeply, receive it in poverty, ponder over it in silence, carry it out in secret and in the joy of being ready to follow it. God's word is welcomed inwardly "with joy inspired by the Holy Spirit" (1 Thess 1: 6) even before it has been put into action. I emphasise the necessity of the following three attitudes of mind for securing the fruitfulness of prayer about the word of God: poverty, silence and readiness. Like Mary — poor, contemplative and ready — who "heard the word of God and did it" (Lk 8:21), and, for this, was proclaimed "blessed".

Another feature of this new prayer is the need of sharing the experience with others, that is the need of praying together, of passing on the riches of the Spirit to one another. I am not speaking of specific prayer groups or movements — with the particular intention of the desire for renewal in the Spirit — but of those daily experiences of community and spontaneous prayer which nowadays seem to be a pressing invitation from the Lord to interior contemplation and evangelical brotherliness.

We can also be sure that a community which prays to the Father "in spirit and in truth" (Jn 4:23), remains solidly united in spite of the inevitable pain of a legitimate divergence of opinion ordained by the Spirit of God. In this sense, it is possible for people to live together in a community — and they should do so — who are very different in age, training and culture and through different inner appreciations of the gospel, by means of the constitutions and chapters and by the Lord's constant appearance in the signs of the times. When prayer is really deep — as a true communion with the Lord a sincere meeting with human beings — the hearts of all necessarily remain peaceful, enlightened and united. In this sense, prayer — when it is a genuine laying oneself open to the Spirit of truth and love — is particularly infallible.

In prayer there are moments which must be absolutely individual. God enters the deepest region of our being and there tells us unspeakable things — which cannot at once be uttered to others — which leave in our hearts the feeling of the cross and an ineffable experience of joy and certain hope. Other people will benefit later — or at once, but in another sphere — by this powerful and exclusive time of alone-ness in the heart. "I will ... bring her into the wilderness, and speak tenderly to her" (Hos 2:16). I think this must have happened in the anguished heart of Jesus in Gethsemani, when he found it necessary to remain absolutely alone with the Father, or only with the three chosen apostles near in spirit. Jesus felt it necessary to be alone after he had won a success or when he was suffering much. "Jesus withdrew again to the hills by himself" (Jn 6:15). "So much the more the report went abroad concerning him; and great multitudes gathered to hear him and to be healed of their infirmities, but he withdrew to the wilderness and prayed" (Lk 5:15).

There are, however, moments of prayer which must be shared with others within a religious community — or in a group in the community — but also with other members of the people of God (priests, other religious, laity). The aspiration and request of people — specially the simplest and the young — to be able to pray with religious is being felt more and more strongly. Thus, they approach contemplative monasteries or different religious communities of the active life: because they feel the need of praying, and they wish to learn how to pray.

I think that one of the most urgent tasks of religious with a view to the evangelisation of peoples and of the evangelical transformation of history may be, today, that of teaching people to pray, starting however from their experience of God. For, one of the most palpable testimonies they expect, today, from religious is to provide men and women of prayer, and to present truly praying communities.

There is another side of prayer which I should like to point out: it is that of a genuine participation in the liturgy, the celebration of the Eucharist, that it may be a true and fruitful immolation and offering of praise in prayer. Everything can be expressed in a single sentence: living and celebrating fundamentally the death and resurrection of Jesus. A genuine celebration of the Eucharist — not only on Sunday but daily — makes us penetrate to the very roots of our conformation with the dead and risen Christ and of our joyful consecration. Let us return to the centre of our liturgical spirituality, the Eucharist. Let us celebrate it every day in the Mass, let us prolong it in the "sacrificium laudis", which is the liturgy of the Hours (Lauds and Vespers particularly), let us absorb it and offer it in strong and prolonged moments of serene, fraternal and purposeful adoration.

One more thing I should like to say about prayer. It is the sense in which our contemplation is deeply human and involved in history. "Let no one think that religious, with their consecration, become divorced from humankind or useless in the earthly city" (LG 46). If silence were a simple evasion of problems, if prayer were nothing but a search for personal comfort or final security, if contemplation were merely abstraction "we should be the most wretched of all men" as St Paul says on the subject of hope. Let us wish, rather, to insist on the fruitfulness for the church of a contemplation which does not dissociate itself from people's problems, but which starts precisely from "their joys, their sorrows and their anxieties" (GS 1), and which seeks to bring humankind into touch with the paschal mystery, since grace works invisibly in the hearts of all (GS 22).

A praying community is a very dutiful community, but its duty is serene and evangelical, that of transforming the world and offering it to God with the ineffable efficacy of the gospel beatitudes (GS 31). Only truly contemplative souls get to the bottom of things, to the heart of problems; and they alone can understand the world and serve it perfectly, for they have learnt first to listen to God. Therefore, the contemplative is most realistic and positive: he has been overtaken by God's reality — most highly loved and experienced on the cross and in the silence of the desert — and now discovers him constantly in those who suffer and hope, who search and love, who work and die for the coming of the kingdom and the building of a more fraternal and human world in which the truth and the justice, the love and the peace, the holiness and grace, the joy and

66

the hope, which have been brought to us by Jesus Christ, may reign.

"Lord, teach us to pray". It seems to me that this may well be the strongest cry of the rising generations. Addressed to the communities, it would mean: "We want to see Jesus" (Jn 12:21), or even: "Show us the Father and we shall be satisfied" (Jn 14:8). In other words they could also say: We want to discover the source of your profession, the secret of your imperturbable balance and your calm, infectious joy, and the root of your generous hospitality and your untiring service to the brethren. In short: we want to know why you are like this, so calm and so bold, so close to us and so different, so marked with the cross and so cheerful, so burdened with work and so serene, so obedient and so free, so alone and so capable of universal love, so apparently distant from the world and so realistic.

The consecrated life is a deep experience of faith in God who first loved us; it is a silent cry to the world — weakened by hatred and violence, but thirsting for peace and unity — a cry which says: "We know and believe the love God has for us. God is Love" (1 Jn 4:16). This very profound and joyful experience of a God who is Love is possible in the measure in which we are silently open to the word of God and the action of the Spirit, in which we have the courage to betake ourselves, alone, into the desert or to climb up the mountain and share with others the fertile solitude of contemplation; in the measure, that is to say, in which we are persons and teachers of prayer, and, still more, in the measure in which we form truly praying communities.

III. Evangelical brotherliness

"Day by day, attending the temple together and breaking bread in their homes, they took food with glad and generous hearts" (Acts 2:46). The witness of an authentic gospel community — nourished by the word of God and the Eucharist, brought into harmony by the Spirit in the simplicity and joy of fraternal love, and driven constantly to the mission and to service — is a very palpable manifestation of the presence of the Lord in the world and one of the strongest invitations to repentance, faith and peaceful fellowship among humans. Therefore, the existence of a real religious community — whether it be large or small — is always a special means of evangelism and the communication of grace. But it is necessary for the community to be "real"; and the first condition is for the Holy Spirit to fill hearts and unite them in the name of the Lord Jesus. Only thus will they make a real family of God's children. A real community involves brotherly hearts. What makes a real community is not the organisation (large or small) nor is it exclusively living together in one single place (be it flat, house or convent). There may be religious who always live together under one roof and who pray together physically but who do not make up a real community. Perhaps one or other (and this would be the saddest thing) finds it easier to live community life outside with a group of people (priests, laity or other religious) who come together to pray and carry out a common pastoral activity. There are many religious who ask themselves: What is my true community? and there are many vocations which are lost or remain paralysed, because they feel that theirs is not a true community.

It is necessary for the Lord to be present; and this requires a deep vision of faith, which guides us all to a common search for the will of God, makes us all humble disciples of his word and also requires a generous capacity for giving our lives. Only the person who is simply and gladly willing to disappear and die is suitable for making up a true community. A human element of primary importance — fundamentally christian and evangelical — must be taken into consideration for the formation of a true community, and that is genuineness in love (cf. Rom 12:9). When we are not sure of the loyalty of the others,

68

we cannot possibly form a community; there will always be an atmosphere of reserve, of constraint and of shyness. In an atmosphere of this sort depth in prayer, joy in work and generosity in mission are impossible.

A genuine community — a group with hearts that are simple and poor, open and sincere, generous and fraternal — presupposes a daily, deep experience of God in prayer. In other words, the religious community (like every other genuine christian community) is born, grows and shows itself in prayer: "They devoted themselves to the apostles' teaching and fellowship, to the breaking of bread and the prayers" (Acts 2:42).

The community implies prayer. If the Spirit does not cry "Abba" forcefully in our hearts, we cannot really feel that we are brothers and sisters. But a genuine prayer is only possible in a genuine community. "If you are offering your gift at the altar, and there remember that your brother has something against you, leave your gift there before the altar; first be reconciled to your brother, and then come and offer your gift" (Mt 5:23-24). The two things — community and prayer — are interwoven and are mutually necessary for their growth. The paschal witness of a praying community is magnificent and infallibly effective. It makes itself known at once not only when its members pray together but also when one of them speaks for God and creates peace from within.

There is in fact a uniform method of entering into the word of God — even though each person keeps the richness of his personality and charism — and a similar method of taking up the cross and offering its fruits to the brethren. It is impossible to escape this law: true conformation with the Christ of Easter — even if made with different temperaments — creates a very deep bond of evangelical brotherliness; and it is infallibly expressed by an unmistakable sign, simplicity and love.

God is extraordinarily simple; complication begins with us. If we are really living in God — absolutely rooted in God — we too shall be simple, cheerful and serene. Otherwise we shall always go on multiplying problems, creating an atmosphere of tension, allowing the essential things of God to escape and clinging on to the temporary things of this world.

Let us form genuine communities! but communities which are deeply animated by the Spirit of God, attentive to the radical demands of Christ crucified and open to the urgent and fundamental needs of humankind. All for the glory of the Father!

A genuine religious community — starting from the most contemplative — always feels itself concerned with the history of peoples and the total salvation of all persons. It is a concrete and immediate way of being "church", "a universal sacrament of salvation". Therefore, every genuine community is always firmly fixed — like any other real ecclesial community — in the heart of the human community. But this it is, only by starting out from its evangelical character and its specific originality as a community of consecrated persons. The more profound and urgent does this incorporation become, the more urgent also is the call to true depth of contemplation (long hours of silence and prayer, solitude and experience of the desert) and to fraternal fellowship within the religious community.

Its openness to the world — by virtue of its mission and evangelism — requires of it a sort of invisible, but real, enclosure, an immediate separation from others so as to be able to meet them and lead them more deeply in God. A genuine religious community — be it small or great, belonging to suburb or the very centre of a town — must always be a prophetic cry of hope, an explicit proclamation of God, an urgent call to repentance, a communication to all of the joy of love, fellowship and encounter.

There remains a final element — which seems to me essential — for the formation of a genuine evangelical community: there must be a leader of fellowship and inspiration. We may call him superior or director, but he is absolutely indispensable. The superior (we use the traditional terminology) is not a person who orders about and makes use of the community: he is, fundamentally, a person who has the ability to train it and inspire it. His authority is essentially a service of fellowship and inspiration. The success of a superior does not lie in having a disciplined community with no problems: it lies, first of all, in offering a real evangelical brotherliness in which all — young and old, leaders and led — seek together the face of God, praise him jointly and communicate him to others in joyful simplicity. Therefore, the superior must have an extraordinary capacity for love, for being radically poor and, in consequence, serene and secure only in the Lord, willing to receive suggestions from the others and to pass on hope to everybody. In a climatae made like that, the co-responsibility and participation of all in a real discernment of the Spirit is not only easy but indispensable.

In a few words; a genuine religious community implies a powerful infusion of the Holy Spirit, a joyful fidelity to the word of God — become a paschal event in the Eucharist — a perfect fitting into the local church, a complete obedience to the charism of its own foundation and a saving presence in the world of the most needy. The model is always the primitive christian community: "They devoted themselves to the apostles' teaching and fellowship, to the breaking of bread and the prayers" (Acts 2:42). "The company of those who believed were of one heart and soul" (Acts 4:32). Such a community does not come about by chance. It involves humble obedience to the Lord, a constant search for his will and an enormous capacity for death. "Unless a grain of wheat falls into the earth and dies, it remains alone; but if it dies, it bears much fruit" (Jn 12:24). A genuine, simple and sincere religious community is always the fruit of the continual death of each of its members and a constant infusion of the Holy Spirit. They are communities which are not born from a simple coincidence of ideals (and still less of an imposed and forced co-existence) but of a deep love of Jesus Christ crucified and a sincere desire to serve the brethren. Only in that way shall we have genuine paschal

71

communities, that is communities which will give a clear, permanent witness of the presence of Jesus risen; for they are communities which pray deeply, love each other sincerely and serve all joyfully, as they always communicate the Good News of salvation.

Conclusion

In order to know what is the testimony of life which is today expected of religious, it is necessary to ask it of the simple folk among our people, without starting from set and artificial schemes. Simple folk have a special gift for getting at the truth. Here also the saying of the gospel is repeated: "I thank thee, Father, Lord of heaven and earth, that thou hast hidden these things from the wise and understanding and revealed them to babes; yes, Father, for such was thy gracious will" (Lk 10:21).

The simple folk of our people want us to be *close* (they need to feel that we really are brothers and sisters and friends), but they want us to be *different:* they need to feel that God is in us, and to experience, in this way, the possibility of a peace, a joy and a hope, which they have been painfully seeking for a long time. Consequently, they want us to be simple and poor, men and women of prayer, witnesses of the love of God, as members of a real evangelical fellowship. Simple folk cannot define poverty, but they live it; they cannot define prayer, but they enjoy it; they do not know what the community is, but they recognise it by intuition and appreciate it.

Someone has lived thoroughly by these values and has left us an example of them (because she was a simple woman of the people): she is Mary, our Mother. She lived in poverty and sang, gratefully, of the joy of her insignificance as a handmaid (Lk 1:48). Mary was deeply contemplative and knew how to keep the things of God in her heart so as to enjoy them at a more convenient time. She was able, with St Joseph and the Child, to make up a true community of love and prayer, of work and enquiry in faith, of pain and hope. More than any one else, she, in the Annunciation, on Calvary and at Pentecost, she made possible — always with the light of the Holy Spirit — the presence of Jesus, the birth of the church and the unbreakable fellowship of humanity with the Father. So, let us put everything in that heart of the poor, contemplative Virgin, the handmaid of the Lord and the Mother of God and of humankind. In that heart we shall learn to be truly poor, to pray well and to build real evangelical communities of fellowship. Is not this the testimony which is expected of us?

OUR LADY'S EASTER

A great portent appeared in heaven,
a woman clothed with the sun, with
the moon under her feet, and on
her head a crown of twelve stars
(Rev 12:1).

HOW important it is in life to be a portent! But not an
empty portent or a sign of death, but rather a sign of life-
giving hope. The present-day world has need of such signs:
the presence and communication of the Easter Christ.
For this reason, we must shine "as lights in the world,
holding fast the word of life" (Phil 2:15-16).

The Assumption of Mary — our Lady's Easter! —
brings us once more face to face with the theme of renewal
and hope. "The Mother of Jesus, glorified in heaven in
body and soul as she now is, is the image and beginning
of the church, which will have its fulfilment in the future
age. So she now shines on earth before the pilgrim people
of God, as a sign of sure hope and consolation, until the
day of the Lord come" (LG 68). These reflections are
pertinent to every form of christian living; but, as I write,
I am thinking particularly of the consecrated life. This
stands in the church for a special manifestation of Easter
renewal and for a sign of the kingdom already present in
history which will be fulfilled when Jesus returns. In it,
therefore, is a serene and lasting invitation to hope.

The Assumption is for Mary what Easter is in the
mystery of Jesus, a consummation of the work of
redemption, a conformation of her frail body with the
glorious body of the Lord, a completion of the mystery
begun in her in the immaculate conception. The centre of
Mary's mystery is the incarnation in her of the Word of
God, but its culmination is her Easter in the Assumption.
Consequently, the Assumption, like Easter for Christ,

is the feast of fulfilment, fulfilment of glorious and grateful fidelity, of the new creation, of sure and consoling hope.

I. Fulfilment of the "Yes" and of the "Magnificat"

The whole of Mary's life was a "Yes" to the Father and a "Magnificat". There were great moments in the joy of her dedication: the Annunciation, the Cross, Pentecost. Yet her true greatness was her daily loyalty to the Father's plan, her radical dedication to the gospel, lived with simplicity and joy of heart. Her poverty was, above all, a serene consciousness of her state as handmaid, hunger for the word of God and for his kingdom, unalterable trust in him for whom nothing is impossible, and immediate readiness for service. The life of Mary was simple: and, without doubt, her "Yes" changed history and her "Magnificat" flooded the world with the joy of redemption. Today we have complicated matters unnecessarily (even within the church and in religious communities). We say "times have changed". Certainly they have. Yet let us not forget that we too — if we want to be true to our specific nature and thoroughly to experience renewal in the Spirit — have the duty of changing things and renewing the times. It is each one's business to write an unpublished page, totally his own, in the history of salvation. Frequently we lose time in looking to see what others have written or, still worse, how and why they have written badly. And meanwhile we neglect to write our own pages. Ultimately, what is essential is, not knowing what is happening in history but rather, seeing where the Lord is passing and what he is asking of us ourselves.

Life has not been given to us for us to preserve it: it has been given to us for the glory of the Father and the service of the brethren. Only thus are we able to save it (Mk 8:35). That requires us to live "with glad and generous hearts" (Acts 2:46) our daily "so be it" to the

Father's will and the expectation of humankind, to the silence of contemplation, to the fruitfulness of the cross and to the joy of fraternal love. All that applies to every baptised person, but it is above all, a requirement of God for the consecrated. A person's greatness is not measured by the splendour of his works, but by lasting, hidden loyalty to his mission, to the word which he has received and carried out. Mary was "blessed" because she said "Yes" (Lk 1:45). True blessedness stands in listening to the word of God and doing it, as did Mary (Lk 11:28). The Assumption is the last "Yes" of our Lady: "I am going to the Father" (cf. Jn 16:28), and it is the greatest sign with which God "has regarded the lowliness of his handmaiden" (Lk 1:48). Because of this the Assumption is also the fulfilment of the "Magnificat".

II.   Image of the new creation

With the "Yes" of Mary a beginning was made of the "last, decisive times" (Heb 1:2). The "Yes" of our Lady marks the fulfilment of the Father's plan, the fullness of the times (Gal 4:4). With the fruitful action of the Holy Spirit who descends upon her (Lk 1:3) "the new creation" begins (Gal 6:15). Mary is thus the image and beginning of the new creation: "Mary, of whom Jesus was born, who is called Christ" (Mt 1:16), for which reason she is the "image and beginning of the church" (LG 68).

In the story of Mary there are three outstanding moments of this new creation. The first is her Immaculate Conception: Mary is, as it were, "moulded and made a new creature by the Holy Spirit" (LG 56). The second is the Annunciation; by her acceptance of the divine message Mary becomes the Mother of Jesus — the New Man, the Saviour, he who takes away the sin of the world — and she dedicates herself totally as handmaid of the Lord to the person and redemptive work of his Son (LG 5). The third is the Assumption: "The immaculate Virgin, kept free from every taint of original sin and having finished her course on earth, was taken up into celestial glory in soul and body, and raised up by the Lord as Queen of the universe, because she was most fully conformed to his Son, the Lord of principalities and the conqueror of sin and death" (LG 59).

The Assumption of Mary is the manifestation of the redeeming work of Jesus and a sign of his decisive victory over sin and death. It is a sign of total freedom. The consecrated life is also a sign of the new creation and a foretaste of its final consummation, provided that it is fully lived as a radical following of Jesus Christ and in the serene joy of sacrifice to the Father and service to the brethren. That is the profound meaning of consecration: a total offering in the style of the cross. The paschal novelty of baptism becomes particularly lucid and concrete in the consecrated life. That life is a clear and enthusiastic testimony to Easter; therefore its mere presence in the world is always a proclamation and a prophecy; it proclaims that Jesus has already come and is alive, and it anticipates in time the serenity and joy of the ultimate kingdom.

The heart of this new creation is love, its source is the cross and its expression is joy. Consequently a sad consecrated life is absurd: it would be like existence without Easter. It is precisely the Assumption of Mary that makes us certain that Easter has been handed down to Christians in its totality. Or rather, that the cross is necessary for entrance into glory (Lk 24:26). But the truth is that our frail body will put on immortality (1 Cor 15:53). This new creation is always given in the Spirit, in the measure with which we allow ourselves to be led by him. In other words, in the measure with which we give ourselves to him who pleads our cause with the Father; that is, in the measure of the depth of our contemplation, of our love for the cross and of our permanent fidelity to the Father's will. A clear sign of this new life in the Spirit is inner balance and an inexhaustible capacity for being joyful. Another very clear sign of this paschal renewal is the experience of a quite deep peace (it is in fact the experience of God dwelling in us) and a permanent readiness to understand, welcome and serve the brethren.

Every baptised person starts eternal life in time (that is the theology of St John and St Thomas Aquinas); and the consecrated life is a prophetic cry that the kingdom of God has reached as far as to us. Thence the hunger for eternity is always aroused: "Come, Lord Jesus" (Rev 22:40). It is the cry of the hope of the whole of creation, sighing for final freedom in the perfect adoption of sons and in the full manifestation of the glory of God (Rom 8:18-25).

III. A sign of certain hope

There are moments in life when we particularly miss someone to remind us of what we already know: for example, that God is our Father and loves us, that we should love each other sincerely, and that Christ our hope is arisen. Let us realise how simple Christianity is and that therefore simple people understand it so well and so quickly. Let us realise, too, that when the christian life is lived intensely it makes men and women very simple. If we feel it to be complicated it is because we have not yet discovered it and have not dared to live it with serene intensity. Simplicity is a sign that one is living in the fullness of love.

Mary's Assumption opens the path for hope to us. How necessary that is at this juncture! We are living in a world which has grown prematurely old and we have good reasons for being worried and unhappy: things are not going well in the world, in the church or in the religious communities. We have, however, a fundamental reason — the only one — for staying cheerful and never losing hope: Christ is risen and prolongs his Easter among us till the end of the age. The mystery of the Assumption of Mary is a call to hope: one day we too shall arrive on high: our Mother has merely preceded us. Now we are in the process of making our way forward in this vale of tears, in her company. The Assumption is a sign of what Christ wishes to do with each one of us, with the whole church and with the whole of humankind: to transform us completely to the pattern and plan of his Father.

To settle down and make ourselves comfortable in time is to sin against hope. We have been created for eternity. We have here no lasting city, but we seek the city which is to come (Heb 13:14). Our true common-wealth is in heaven (Phil 3:20). There we shall receive abundant joy (Mt 25:34). Meanwhile let us live "awaiting our blessed hope" (Tit 2:13). Our fundamental attitude as pilgrims is not just to suffer nostalgia for the good things of eternity and to despise or ignore temporal good things and other things of this world, but rather to live in a state of watchfulness, that is in an attitude of prayer, practising charity and bringing our talents to fruition, in the ardent and active expectation of our Lord's coming. When the temptation to adapt ourselves to the age, or to go to sleep, comes to us, there is someone — the Spirit of God dwelling in us — who cries within us: "The Lord is already come" (cf. Mt 25:6), or even "The Teacher is here and is calling for you" (Jn 11:28).

Hoping is not merely waiting. It is essentially moving towards the meeting with the Lord who is building up the kingdom every day, and every day writing a new page in the history of humanity. Hoping is being sure that Jesus is coming and for that reason taking together the path towards the joy of the ultimate meeting: "we shall always be with the Lord" (1 Thess 4:17), and being faithful to our mission, as we make our efforts to change the world according to the pattern of the gospel.

The whole christian existence, being a paschal experience, is a cry of hope: "Christ my hope is arisen" (Easter sequence), and the consecrated life — stripping oneself

79

of everything so as radically to follow Christ crucified —
is a prophetic proclamation of hope: Christ alone matters.
"For his sake I have suffered the loss of all things, and
count them as refuse, in order that I may gain Christ and
be found in him" (Phil 3:8-9).

In our times — of excessive euphoria about temporal
goods or of tragic weariness and pessimism about human
problems — how little hope there is! And how much good
it does us, instead, to think of the mystery of Mary's
Assumption — our Lady's Easter — as a "sign of certain
hope".

This is the feast of the fullness of joy. Therefore it
is, as the name suggests, the feast of the "Magnificat"
(the liturgy reminds us of it in the gospel of the day). So,
it is the feast of the completeness of the "Yes": and the
"Yes" made our Lady fundamentally blessed (Lk 1:45);
it is the feast of the new creation and the celebration of
the hope which does not disappoint us (Rm 5:5); for the
love of God has reached its fullness in the poverty and
fidelity of Mary in the Assumption. Wherefore it is our
Lady's Easter.

THE MISSIONARY ASPECT OF THE RELIGIOUS LIFE

> As the Father has sent me, even so send I you (Jn 21:1).
>
> Go into all the world and preach the gospel to the whole creation (Mk 16:15).
>
> If I preach the gospel, that gives me no ground for boasting. For necessity is laid upon me. Woe to me if I do not preach the gospel! (1 Cor 9:16).

THESE remarks apply to every Christian. The whole church is essentially missionary, evangelical and saving. Yet, how are we to discover and put into practice the deeply missionary aspect of the consecrated life? I think we should insist on these three points: Christ, the church, the world. The religious life is distinguished by a special following of Christ, by a specific way of living the life of the church, and by a special call to transform the world according to the spirit of the Beatitudes (LG 31).

I. The following of Christ

Baptismal consecration has already incorporated us all "in the school of Christ". But religious consecration involves a special way of conforming to Christ, in his being and mission, in his death and resurrection. It involves a deep assimilation to the filial soul of Christ "glorifier of the Father and saviour of men". For Christ the only way to love the Father is by seeking his glory, showing the Father's secrets to humankind and dying on the cross

F

as a ransom for all. Christ is the Father's Son made man, the Lord of history and the Saviour of the world.

Loyalty to the plan of the Father, "who desires all men to be saved and to come to the knowledge of the truth" (1 Tim 2:4) requires in Christ an essentially missionary and sacrificial attitude. Christ came to save the whole human person and all humankind. Therefore he preached the gospel of the kingdom, inviting to repentance and faith (Mk 1:15). Therefore he embraced the cross and, of his own accord, gave up his life (Jn 10:17-18). The radical following of Christ involves in consecrated souls absolute loyalty to the Father's plan; this is the explicit will of the Father: that everyone shall be saved. This is the central point of the gospel: "God sent the Son into the world, not to condemn the world, but that the world might be saved through him" (Jn 3:17).

There are three aspects of the following of Christ which strongly mark the missionary character of consecrated souls:

1. *The Easter Christ*

Let us strongly conform ourselves to the *Easter Christ*, that is, to the Christ of the covenant, to Christ Jesus "whom God made our wisdom, our righteousness and salvation and redemption" (1 Cor 1:30). In the missionary Christ the essential is not the immediate transmission of the message, but the redemption which works through the shedding of his blood. There were many to listen to and accept his words; not all were to accept the salvation which he came to offer to them.

In the missionary Christ there is a trait which I am particularly concerned to emphasise: his contemplative silence, his self-annihilation in accepting through obedience the death on the cross (Phil 2:8).

Generally when we think of the missionary nature of the church — or of the missionary character of the religious life — we at once find we are thinking of apostolic activity or the prophetic function of those who proclaim the Good News of salvation. We think little of those who, like Mary, in contemplative silence beget the "Word of salvation", or, again like Mary, collaborate in the work of universal salvation through the fruition of the cross and of death. The saying of Jesus: "Unless a grain of wheat falls into the earth and dies, it remains alone; but, if it dies, it bears much fruit" (Jn 12:24) is valid here too. That is why a contemplative nun who prayed much and sacrificed herself much, St Thérèse of the Child Jesus, has become the patron of the missions.

2. Christ the Prophet

Let us conform ourselves in a special way to *Christ the Prophet*. The religious life is a particular expression in the church of the prophetic function of Christ, with word and witness. The mere existence of a genuine religious community — praying and fraternal — is an evident manifestation of the kingdom of God and the revelation of a loving God who invites us to repentance, reconciliation and salvation. In addition the Spirit sends us to bear the Good News "to the end of the earth" (Acts 1:8).

Special conformation with Christ the Prophet involves three things: deep assimilation of the whole gospel, personal and communal putting into practice of the word received (Lk 11:27), and universal proclamation of the salvation brought to fulfilment by Jesus. A genuine religious community is an obvious sign of the presence of the paschal Christ and an urgent invitation to repentance and faith. The missionary character of the religious life

83

does not get measured so much by the immediate effectiveness of the spoken word or the activity carried out, as by the evident manifestation and communication of Christ the Saviour, brought about by means of a community which remains united in "the apostles' teaching and fellowship, in the breaking of bread and the prayers" (Acts 2:42).

3. *The poor, chaste and obedient Christ*

Finally, let us follow *the poor, chaste and obedient Christ* as far as the death on the cross. The missionary character of the evangelical counsels is very clear. We have left everything to follow Christ and to serve humankind for its salvation. Here the essential is the oblation of our whole life to Christ for the sake of the kingdom, to bear witness to it as present, to proclaim it prophetically as definitive and to help to build it every day in this world for the glory of the Father. The vows, if they are carried out with sincerity and joy in the Spirit, make us free and enable us to serve our brothers and sisters generously. Yet, above all, they are a manifestation of our radical offering to the Father by means of Jesus Christ in the Holy Spirit. They involve annihilation and dying; but they are, above all, the expression of a paschal covenant and fullness of life.

If the vows are lived out in a serene context of love — a joyful sacrifice to the Father and a generous offering to the brethren — they acquire an extraordinary missionary power. They make us ready to live only for the sake of the salvation of humankind, but above all, they show to the world that God is love and sent his Son into the world so that we may live through him (1 Jn 4:7-10) and that the love of God has been put into our hearts by means of the Holy Spirit who has been given to us (Rom 5:5).

II. On the mystery of the church

"Now you are the body of Christ and individually members of it" (1 Cor 12:27).

The consecrated life has meaning only within a church, the people of God, an essentially missionary fellowship. "I am the true vine ... abide in me, and I in you ... . I chose you and appointed you that you should go and bear fruit and that your fruit should abide" (Jn 15:1, 4, 16). It is the fruit of personal sanctification, of the conversion and salvation of humankind, of universal reconciliation in Christ.

The consecrated life is a particular way of being and actualising the missionary church. It shares the energy of the Holy Spirit, who dwells in it and spurs it to incorporate itself into the world as "universal sacrament of salvation" (LG 48; AG 1) and to proclaim its witness of the resurrection of Christ to the ends of the earth. But the religious life brings it into being from the starting point of its own original charism. That requires absolute loyalty to its specific identity, to its own existence. That means that the missionary character of the consecrated life inevitably has its origin in its own consecration and mission. An exclusively contemplative life — if lived fully in the church — is marvellously and fundamentally missionary. It goes more deeply and is more permanent than apostolic activity itself.

In the church there are specifically missionary vocations. So there spring up, for example, various institutes and congregations, providentially raised up by the Holy Spirit for the missions. There are consecrated souls who have chosen a particular way of following Christ because they have experienced a special call to leave everything and betake themselves to distant lands to proclaim there the Good News of Jesus. That does not arise from a spirit of novelty or adventure, but from an interior demand of the Spirit. They must be discovered and encouraged, and prayer must be made to the Lord for them to be multiplied. Above all at this moment, it is urgent to apply the Lord's word: "The harvest is plentiful, but the labourers are few; pray therefore the Lord of the harvest to send out labourers into his harvest" (Lk 10:2).

At times a sort of weariness arises in the church. There exists also a certain concern about the very sense and validity of being a missionary. The deviations and excesses perpetrated at particular moments in particular countries do not take away the essential reality of missions. Specific forms of proselytism — which seemed to suppress indigenous cultures — are certainly no longer in use. The Council, when speaking of the missionary character of the church, says: "Its activity has this outcome, that every grain of good found in the heart and mind of human beings or in the particular rites and cultures of peoples must not be lost, but is to purified, elevated and perfected for the glory of God, the confusion of the devil and the happiness of humankind" (LG 17). "The pilgrim church is by its nature missionary, since it draws its origin from the mission of the Son, and from the mission of the Holy Spirit, according to God the Father's plan" (AG 2).

I should like to emphasise three aspects of this essentially missionary church and, in her, of the missionary character of the religious life:

a) There is a mission which comes into being, in depth and urgent maturity of faith, even in countries which have not yet been evangelised and where the church has emerged officially as a community of believers in Christ. The church is constantly "sent" into this world, strongly spurred on by the Holy Spirit to penetrate it and change it. The church is not a static community, but a dynamic community of salvation. The mission here consists of continuing the proclamation of Christ and the demands of his kingdom, daily calling to conversion and to the maturity of faith, creating deep, fraternal and zealous communities, capable

86

of transforming the world, of making it more human and more divine, and of offering it to the Father.

It is the "caring" missionary who fundamentally inspires the life and activity of the church at various levels wherever it is found. The essential mission of the church, like that of Christ, is explicitly to proclaim the kingdom and to save humankind completely. In this sense, prayer and the cross, life hidden in God and catechistic activity, scholastic teaching and works of mercy, acquire an essentially missionary character: it is the church which goes out from the cenacle and into the world, so as to proclaim God's wonders and accomplish the universal salvation of all. Whatever may be the practical manner of a religious life, it must necessarily have this missionary character.

b) There is also a missionary concern to take to other places and other countries the Good News of salvation, Jesus' message, and the call to enter his kingdom. To this may be ascribed the urgency of specific missionary vocations (in the classical, traditional sense): "Every one who calls on the name of the Lord will be saved. But how are men to call upon him in whom they have not believed? And how are they to believe in him of whom they have never heard? And how are they to hear without a preacher? And how can men preach unless they are sent?" (Rom 19:13-15).

Unfortunately, as we have said before, there are factors which have caused a lessening of interest in and enthusiasm for these evangelical forms of missionary life. We should ask ourselves whether the Lord is not calling us, in a new and urgent way, to free ourselves, to leave all and arrange to share the lot of the many brethren who are living in darkness and seeking the light, experiencing sadness and death but longing for joy and life, feeling that they are orphans but sighing ardently for someone to speak to them of the Father.

    c) Lastly, there is an aspect of the missionary life which it is urgent to emphasise: it is the silent and fruitful sharing — by means of the joy of loyalty, of deep contemplation and the cross — in all the church's missionary activity. This is where consecrated souls like Mary, at the foot of the cross or in the contemplative intimacy of the upper room, have a privileged position and a providential mission. The aim of the mission is always the same: for Christ to be proclaimed and for the whole of humanity to be saved through him. For consecrated souls — who have decisively united their lives with Christ the Saviour of the world — missionary urgency becomes specially strong and impelling: Christ requires it, the church asks for it, and it is hoped for by men and women ransomed in hope (Rom 8:24) and called to reproduce the image of Jesus Christ, the first-born of many brethren (Rom 8:29).

III. With the spirit of the Beatitudes

The consecrated life is distinguished by a special way of living the gospel life, i.e., practically speaking, the Beatitudes. This is affirmed by the Council in outlining the unmistakable identity of religious: "By their condition (they) testify in a splendid and singular way that the world cannot be transformed and offered to God without the spirit of the beatitudes" (LG 31). The religious life takes its place too in relation to the world: it does not undervalue it, it does not condemn it, nor does it run away from it. It simply separates itself from it so as to save it as Christ did in the desert and on the cross. Christ did not come to condemn the world but to save it (Jn 3:17) and he did not ask the Father to take his disciples out of the world but to keep them from the evil one (Jn 17:15). The evangelising mission fits them into the world — as privileged witnesses of the kingdom — in a new way: "As thou hast sent me into the world, so I have sent them into the world" (Jn 17:18).

However, the relationship with the world is always planned with the purpose of an evangelising and saving mission: to witness to the kingdom, to ensure Jesus' presence and to call men and women to repentance and faith. The Beatitudes lay down the manner of living and working. For this reason the missionary side of the religious life should be sought more in the lines of its religious being rather than of its activity. The words of Paul VI in *Evangelii nuntiandi* need to be read again: "Let the religious, in their turn, find a privileged means of effective evangelism in the consecrated life. With the intimate nature of their being itself they take their place in the church's efforts, athirst for the absolute reality of God and called to holiness as she is. They are a testimony of this holiness and the incarnation of the church as she wills to abandon herself to the radicalism of the Beatitudes. Their lives make them a sign of being completely at the disposal of God, the church and their brethren" (EN 69). I wish to underline these ideas of the Pope's:

a) The religious life has in itself an evangelising and missionary character:

— because it is a witness to the absolute reality of God and to the holiness to which we are all called in the church. It is, consequently, a call to repentance,

— because it is a sign of complete readiness for the service of God, the church and the brethren. Consequently, it is a manifestation of the joy of love, and a powerful invitation to live in the fullness of charity. Charity is the essence of christian living, the standard by which we shall be judged

(Mt 25:31-46) and the most perfect and lasting of the theological virtues (1 Cor 13:8-13). The consecrated life is an eminently God-centred life, an experience of faith, a communication of hope and a joyful covenant of charity,

— because, by way of the silent witness of poverty and detachment, the deep joy of consecrated chastity and the active and mature self-abandonment of obedience, it is a constant influence in the world and the church herself. It is a witness which even non-Christians of good faith notice.

b) This religious life has its place in the dynamism of the church athirst for the absolute reality of God and called to holiness, and, at the same time, essentially sent into the world to preach the gospel to every creature, and to bring about in Christ the salvation of the whole of humankind.

c) Thanks to religious consecration many men and women willingly and freely leave everything and go to proclaim the gospel to the ends of the earth. Yet there is also a missionary power springing from the silence and prayer, the penitence and sacrifice, of consecrated souls. I wish to emphasise afresh — and this is also the Holy Father's intention — the force and missionary efficacy of the consecrated life.

Perhaps the true essence of the missionary aspect of the consecrated life is found here, in deep-rooted loyalty to Jesus Christ and his gospel, in profound assimilation to the Beatitudes, and in absolute readiness to live "in genuine love" (Rom 12:9) in all its aspects and requirements (God and creature, contemplation and the cross, sacrifice and service).

Living in the spirit of the Beatitudes is absorbing deeply the missionary spirit of Jesus. It is entering into a profound experience of God and the urgency of his kingdom. It is recognising the cry of men and women who want, and hope for, salvation. It is feeling the immediate urgency of enlightening them in the faith, animating them in the hope, and saving them in the charity of Christ who died for the salvation of all.

The person who lives thoroughly by the Beatitudes does not feel happy in isolation, but tries to make others happy. He knows that true happiness is found only in the saving cross of Christ. He who lives thoroughly and tranquilly by the Beatitudes shows clearly before all the faithful that the good things of heaven are already present in this world, as witnesses to the new, eternal life won with Christ's redemption, and he anticipates the future resurrection and the glory of the heavenly kingdom (LG 44). All this is an essential part of the missionary side of the religious life.

Such is the missionary strength of the consecrated life itself that the Council says: "The religious life must be promoted from the earliest implanting of the church, for it not only brings precious and indispensable help to missionary activity, but by a more intimate consecration to God, made within the church, it shows and expresses quite clearly the intimate nature of the christian vocation" (AG 18).

Living the life of the Beatitudes is absorbing the poor and merciful soul of Jesus, feeling with him the hunger and thirst for righteousness, forcing oneself to be a true peacemaker by the silence of the cross, having a pure and upright heart so as to see God, and enjoying the fruits of persecution for righteousness' sake. Thus are enlarged the horizons of charity, and the kingdom of God is thrown open to the redemption of all people of good will.

What shall we do for the religious life to fulfil its missionary role intensely and joyfully? I would mention these three points briefly:

a) We must have an intense *experience of the life of*

prayer so that it will help us to penetrate deeply into the universal saving plan of the Father, into the redeeming mission of Jesus who was "sent by the Father" for the salvation of the world, and into the unceasingly renewing and sanctifying activity of the Holy Spirit. We must contemplate, in great moments of silence and prayer, the figure of Jesus, Prophet, Missionary and Saviour, and we must absorb deeply his teachings (particularly the Sermon on the Mount — the Beatitudes! — the parables of the kingdom and the discourses of the last supper).

b) We must discover ever more deeply the mystery of the church "universal sacrament of salvation", in its essential nature and missionary urgency today, listening, on the one hand, to the universal command of Christ: "Go therefore and make disciples of all nations, baptising them ..." (Mt 28:19) and, on the other, to the agonising loneliness and expectation of the folk who cry: "How can I (understand), unless some one guides me?" (Acts 8:31).

Within the heart of this church we must penetrate ever more deeply into the missionary and evangelical dynamism of our own religious being, of our specific identity and original charism, as a special way of radically following Christ, living the life of the Beatitudes and constantly proclaiming the kingdom.

c) We must create *authentic communities,* whose mere presence is an evident sign of the arrival of the kingdom and a quiet call to repentance and faith; communities characterised by the joy and simplicity of fraternal love, by a true sense of prayer and the fruitfulness of contemplation, and by a special presence of the spirit of evangelical fellowship and missionary dynamism. We like to call them "paschal communities", that is to say, paschal communities where the lively, working presence of the Easter Christ and the transforming prayer of the Spirit of Pentecost are felt. They are essentially praying, fraternal and missionary communities.

Conclusion

I would like to end by remembering the figure of Mary, the beginning and image of the missionary church. The power of the Spirit overshadowed her mysteriously in the Annunciation and Pentecost. Her contemplative inner life and her fullness of faith, her path of hope in the Visitation, her joyful immolation at the cross, and her spirit of fellowship and prayerful waiting at Pentecost inspire the evangelical energy of the church and throw a strong light on the missionary side of the consecrated life. The Word was born in Mary. In presenting him — at the Visitation, in the Nativity and in the Temple — she "kept all these things (and pondered them) in her heart" (Lk 2:19-51). At the climax of the paschal mystery of the Son — when Christ reconciled the world with the Father with the death on the cross, and gave his life for the redemption of all — Mary is there, calm and strong, cooperating with her silence and inner martyrdom in the redemptive work of Christ. Pentecost marks the beginning of the missionary church: its spirit of fellowship, its contemplative attitude and its hope springing from the cross were to act in such a way that the apostles — the first missionaries — would go everywhere to preach the gospel of the kingdom (Mk 16:20), would be witnesses of the resurrection to the furthest ends of the earth (Acts 1:8; 2:32; 4:33) and that their word would be received as the word of God even in the midst of great tribulation "with joy inspired by the Holy Spirit" (1 Thess 1:6).

Let us now leave in the heart of Mary — the Virgin of contemplative silence, the Virgin of the Cross, full of hope, the Virgin of the willing and redemptive giving, the Virgin specially loved by the Father and consecrated by the Spirit, the Mother of Christ and the church — let us leave with her the responsibility and the grace of the missionary character of consecrated souls.

THE RENEWAL OF THE RELIGIOUS LIFE AND THE HOPE OF THE YOUNG

> If anyone is in Christ, he is a new creation; the old has passed away, behold, the new has come (2 Cor 5:17).

> Be renewed in the spirit of your minds, and put on the new nature, created after the likeness of God in righteousness and true holiness (Eph 4:23-24).

Introduction

I INTEND to deal with this subject in the context of the "paschal church" not only because I happen to be writing at Easter-time, but also because the three terms which, in this subject, refer to the religious life clearly require it: they are renewal, hope, and youth.

It is significant that the expression "paschal church" was used by the Latin-American bishops at Medellin just at the time when they were trying to "reply to the strong and legitimate pastoral pleas of the young, in which we are bound to recognise a call from God". The evangelical reply to the "pleas of the young" and the "call from God" is this: "that in Latin America the image of a church, genuinely poor, missionary and paschal, free of all temporal power and boldly determined on the liberation of every person and the whole of humankind, be presented ever more clearly" (Med 5, 15).

Everything brings us to think of the "paschal renewal" which was brought to us by Jesus, the "New Man", in the resurrection by which the Father made us "born anew to a living hope" (1 Pet 1:3). Let us realise this "paschal renewal" in the religious life which, being by definition a very special and radical *sequela Christi* in the "search for perfect charity" (PC 1; ET 1, 4, 7, 12), involves a progressive conformation, begun in baptism, to the dead and risen Christ, so that in him and through him "we too may walk in newness of life" (Rom 6:4). The "special consecration" of the religious life "has its roots in baptismal consecration and expresses it more fully" (ET 4; PC 5).

But the religious life — the Spirit's gift to the church — must be fully lived within a paschal church, which, at the same time, is a presence and communication of the risen Christ, a sign and instrument of fraternal and divine fellowship (LG 1) and a universal sacrament of salvation (LG 48; GS 45; AG 1 and 5). The religious life is a privileged way — with the privileges of love, of the cross and of service — of being church. Living the religious life with sincerity is living with growing intensity the mystery of the church. Consequently, every renewal in the religious life requires a deep experience of Christ crucified (1 Cor 2:2), of Christ the initiator of all creation and the first-born from the dead (Col 1:15-18), who lives in the church to save the entire human race: "Christ in you, the hope of glory" (Col 1:27).

A true renewal of the religious life happens always from within a church which, with the life-giving power of the Spirit, "continually goes forward by the way of penitence and renewal" (LG 8). It happens, that is to say, from within a church which unceasingly tries to be faithful to Christ and to humankind. "With the power of the gospel, (the Holy Spirit) makes the church young again, constantly renews her and leads her to perfect union with her Spouse" (LG 4). Consequently, any renewal in the religious life — slow, profound, continuous — is the work of the Spirit who "makes all things new"; it requires a real conversion, involves a deep love for the church and thirsts for holiness, the desire for contemplation and service and the communication of joy and hope.

When we speak of the "paschal church" — within which the renewal of the religious life and the hope of the young make sense — we mean particularly the "church of the kenosis" (Phil 2:5-10), that is, the church of self-annihilation and exaltation, the church of death and resurrection, the church of the cross and of hope, the church of the Incarnation, poverty and service, the church of the grain of wheat which dies in order to grow and bear ears of corn (Jn 12:24).

The young love this church particularly: a church which is poor, fraternal and ready to serve, a church of contemplation and prophecy, the sacramental presence of the Christ of Easter, who came exclusively to fulfil the Father's will and give his life for his friends, to reconcile the world with the Father and establish peace among peoples, to proclaim the kingdom of truth, righteousness and love, and to call men and women to repentance and faith.

When we think of the hopes of the young faced with this church — and, consequently faced with the religious life as a privileged way of being and expressing the church — we think that there are two ways of shattering or killing this hope:

— by being too fearful so that renewal does not even start or goes much too slowly. Really that means a lack of trust in the permanent presence of the risen Christ (Mt 28:20) and too little compliance with the Spirit, who is calling and encouraging, inviting inwardly and transforming;

— by being too bold (certainly not with the boldness of the Spirit) and seeking change primarily for the sake of change, without distinguishing the essential from the accidental, the new in Christ from the simply new and fashionable, or without taking notice of the divine teaching about fundamental changes. That is the "audacity of some arbitrary changes" of which Paul VI speaks (ET 2).

Fundamentally it is the same thing: people have not in this matter taken a position of calm and humble listening to the word of God, ready to follow the promptings of the Spirit; they have been too eager to follow the

G

prudence of the flesh and the demagogic yearning for novelty. Instead of being lived in the dynamism proper for paschal renewal, the religious life has remained paralysed in the "strait-jacket of formalism" (ET 12) and has tended to dissipate itself in a "world of secularisation" (ET 3).

The sense of the really new in Christ is missing, and so is that which leads to the really new, i.e., conversion. Thus fruitfulness and patience, simplicity and joy, understanding and hope are all missing. Further, the religious communities have been invaded by pessimism and gloom, mistrust and timidity, painful division between those who run too fast and those who have not yet started to move. There is no poverty and prayer, no humility and discussion, no sincere love and complete readiness to the promptings of the Spirit.

I. Renewal in the Spirit

"We rejoice in our sufferings, knowing that suffering produces endurance, and endurance produces character, and character produces hope, and hope does not disappoint us, because God's love has been poured into our hearts through the Holy Spirit who has been given to us" (Rom 5:3-5).

Let us take from St Paul's text these double pairings: the cross and hope, the love of God and the Holy Spirit.

A paschal church is "a sacrament of the love of God for human beings", meaning that it expresses and passes on to men and women a "God who is love" (cf. 1 Jn 4:8), a faithful God who has become close to us and intimate with us in Jesus Christ. The Council puts this very well: "Everything good which the people of God can offer to the human family during its time of pilgrimage on earth, springs from the fact that the church is the 'universal sacrament of salvation' which unveils and at the same time realises the mystery of God's love towards his creatures" (GS 45).

The religious life bears witness — at personal and community level — to this same love of God for men and women. It is a deep experience of the faithfulness of God made palpable through the brethren. Therefore, when it is thoroughly lived, in the simplicity and joy of every day, it makes a great impression on the young and influences them. The young easily follow great individuals who live simply, strong persons who live cheerfully, sincere men and women who "love without dissimulation" (Rom 12:9 AV).

Renewal of the religious life imposes at once the obligation of loyalty to the Spirit. He speaks to us by way of the unchangeable word of God and the extremely changeable course of history. There is need of much inner poverty and a great capacity for contemplation in order to treat this word as new every day, to welcome it among us and to put it into practice generously. The world expects us to be witnesses of a kingdom already in being and prophets of hope.

Any genuine renewal of the religious life must induce us to live in the Spirit in accordance with the requirements of love and to express them in our lives every day. More than any one else, the young repeat sincerely: "We believe the love God has for us" (1 Jn 4:16).

It is possible for communities to be in a state of tension. It is a tension of the Spirit, putting them into a situation of crisis so that they may ripen in faith, become alive to hope and live together in charity. But there cannot be communities divided and discordant, radically disunited and obstinately conscious of absolute possession of the truth, cold communities in which love seems to be dead and the Spirit quenched (1 Thess 5:19).

The young of today are particularly sensitive to love in its dual character: as a joyful sacrifice to the Father and a generous giving to the brethren. The religious life is renewed, under the action of the Holy Spirit, in this two-fold requirement of love, as an offering and as a service. What opens the ways of hope to the young is not a com-

99

fortable, superficial life — which is always fundamentally a "life according to the flesh" — but rather an austere life "in the Spirit". St John's words are always valid; "I write to you, young men, because you are strong, and the word of God abides in you, and you have overcome the world" (1 Jn 2:14). Even more valid are Jesus' demands: "You lack one thing; go, sell what you have, and give to the poor, and you will have treasure in heaven; and come, follow me" (Mk 10:21).

Consequently, the renewal of the religious life — if it is really meant to satisfy the aspirations of the young — must always be undertaken in the sincerity of the gospel and in the power of the Spirit: living in a new way a life of radical dedication to the Father in consecration, of sweet experience of God in prayer and of the glorious meaning of the paschal cross.

1. Consecration

This is a total and final dedication to Christ, poor, chaste, and obedient unto death on the cross. "For their sake I consecrate myself, that they also may be consecrated in truth" (Jn 17:19; ET 7). It is a "complete and irreversible" consecration to Christ, through the ministry of the church, to the praise of the glory of God (Eph 1:6) and for the salvation of humankind.

The new way of living by the evangelical counsels not only does not lessen their demands, but deepens and broadens them. It nails us more firmly to the cross. We are bound to bring into prominence the kenotic aspect of the vows, that is the meaning of the joyful sacrifice to the Father by means of the deep sharing in the paschal mystery of Jesus. It is from this that is derived their social character and their capability of transforming and building up history.

The young are particularly sensitive to poverty, but it must be genuine, simple and cheerful poverty, and poverty, to be genuine must be lived simply and shown, rather than proclaimed in the style of a demagogue. True poverty is hunger for God and need of prayer, lack of personal security, trust in him for whom nothing is impossible, real detachment from material wealth, freedom in clashes with temporal powers, and unselfish solidarity with those who suffer hunger and wretchedness, loneliness, injustice and oppression. We must "hear the cry of the poor from the depth of their personal indigence and collective misery" (ET 16-22; Med 14). "An inarticulate clamour comes from the throats of millions of persons who ask of their pastors a liberation which comes to them from nowhere. 'You listen to us now in silence but we hear the cry that rises from your suffering'" (Med 14:2).

Poverty is a way of finding Christ in one's brother and sister (Mt 25), but, above all, it is a way of taking part in the "generosity of Jesus Christ who, though he was rich, yet for our sake he became poor that you might become rich" (2 Cor 8:9).

Consecrated chastity is a special way of sharing in the paschal mystery of Christ in his death and in his resurrection. It must be lived as a joyful expression of a love which is at once sacrifice to the Father and ability to serve the brethren. "When it is really lived with the gaze fixed on the kingdom of heaven, it frees the human heart and turns itself into "a symbol and stimulus of charity and a special source of fruitfulness in the world" (ET 14; LG 42). It does not destroy human love, but gives it an inner and divine completion, makes it deeper and more sincere, simpler and more spontaneous, more universal and permanent. True friendship, in consecrated celibacy, acquires solidity and the fruitfulness of the cross. It is Easter being celebrated in our lives.

Mature and responsible obedience, too, is a particular conformation with Christ, the Servant of Yahweh "who became obedient unto death, even the death of the cross" (Phil 2:8). It implies great interior freedom: "The Father loves me, because I lay down my life, that I may take it up again. No one takes it from me, but I lay it down of

101

my own accord" (Jn 10:17-18). This involves a clear understanding of God's plan: "I have come down from heaven, not to do my own will, but the will of him that sent me" (Jn 6:38). It involves even more, an attitude of deep faith and a generous dedication to the cross: "Not my will, but thine, be done" (Lk 22:42). Christ learnt obedience in the school of suffering (Heb 5:8).

2. Experience of God in prayer

One of the characteristics of the young today is the search for the inner life, the love of contemplation, the desire for God, not as an escape from history, from the apostolic mission and from service to the brethren, but rather as a way of realising more genuinely the historical aspect of their lives, and of their mission as apostles, prophets and witnesses, and the urgency of an effort for freedom in the face of their fellow creatures and society.

"The Lord has given me the tongue of those who are taught, that I may know how to sustain with a word him that is weary. Morning by morning he wakens, he wakens my ear to hear as those that are taught" (Is 50:4). Only persons of fertile silence — true contemplatives — are capable of saying a new word every day. Only persons of prayer recognise the passing of the Lord in history every day; only they can understand the mystery of man in the light of the incarnate Word (GS 22) and read the "signs of the times" in the perspective of salvation.

The renewal of the religious life is trying to realise itself by a deepening of the inner life. In the religious communities there is a hunger for more authentic prayer. It is also worthy of note that the general chapters held in the last years and months have been specially characterised by the priority given to prayer. In this indeed may be recognised a clear invitation and an action by the Spirit of the inner life, who, on the one hand, "will guide (us) into all truth" (Jn 6:13) and, on the other, "helps us in our weakness, for we do not know how to pray as we

102

ought, but the Spirit himself intercedes for us with sighs too deep for words" (Rom 8:26).

In the new generations of religious, there is evidence of particular insistence on — and consequently a strong invitation by the Spirit to — these three topics: life of prayer, sense of community, and missionary spirit.

Again we dwell upon the experience of God in prayer. There is an experience of God which is given to us in the daily march of history or in the troubled existence of peoples and nations. Men and women of faith feel here, with relative ease and with gratitude, the revelation of a God who is love and requires the active effort of our love in reply. Religious are palpable and credible witnesses of this love. For the same reason, renewal demands "strong moments" of experience of God in the desert: moments of absolute solitude, of exclusive prayer and of radical and complete dedication to the word in silence. No one can be a genuine witness of Easter, a calm proclaimer of the kingdom and a bold prophet of hope, who does not know how to enjoy the manifestation of God in the desert, or to speak with him in the Tabernacle of Meeting "face to face, as a man speaks to his friend" (Ex 33:11).

3. Meaning of the paschal cross

We have already said that the consecrated life, lived in full in the inner life of love, always involves a kenotic aspect of Easter: incarnation, poverty, service, annihilation, obedience unto death, even the death on the cross (Phil 2:5-11).

We now stress the fact that the rising generations are looking for an authentic following of Christ crucified in the religious life: "If any man would come after me, let him deny himself and take up his cross daily and follow me" (Lk 9:23).

Among the young — perhaps because they have been disillusioned by the wise and strong of this world, but I believe by the providential inspiration of the Holy Spirit who is working in them powerfully — there is the glorious discovery of the fact that in Christ crucified there dwells "the power of God and the wisdom of God to those who are called" (1 Cor 1:24).

Among religious, as soon as the following of Jesus has been seriously begun, the experience of pain and the cross shows itself. This is a grace; it does not destroy them, but strengthens them and makes them happy. Furthermore, it prepares them to share in their innermost lives the sufferings of Jesus in their brothers and sisters. Therefore, a true renewal of the religious life — such as really kindles and impresses the young — always comes about by way of a sincere and silent search for greater austerity, a more radical loyalty to the gospel and a joyful sharing of the Lord's cross. All this, however, is in the calm and fruitful dimension of Easter, that is with a sense of joy and solidarity illuminated by hope: "I rejoice in my sufferings for your sake, and in my flesh I complete what is lacking in Christ's afflictions for the sake of his body, that is, the church" (Col 1:24), "But far be it from me to glory except in the cross of our Lord Jesus Christ, by which the world has been crucified to me, and I to the world" (Gal 6:14).

II. Witnesses of Easter renewal

"You shall receive power when the Holy Spirit has come upon you and you shall be my witnesses (Acts 1:8).

The religious life is a joyful proclamation of the kingdom, an explicit testimony of the new life in the Spirit, and a prophetic cry of the resurrection of Jesus. For the young to believe in the religious life, renewal must come by a genuine process of inner conversion, which has the effect of creating poor, praying, fraternal and missionary communities and of causing deep experience of God to be shown in the simplicity and joy of every-day life. A text of the Acts describes the paschal testimony of the primitive church — strongly invaded by the Spirit of Pentecost — and it synthesises its essential characteristics and the elementary requirement of conversion. Peter summarises the content of his Easter preaching thus: "Let all the house of Israel know assuredly that God has made him both Lord and Christ, this Jesus whom you crucified" (Acts 2:36). At once, under the influence of the Holy Spirit, comes the reaction of the hearers: "What shall we do?" And Peter replies: "Repent, and be baptised every one of you in the name of Jesus Christ ... and you shall receive the gift of the Holy Spirit" (Acts 2:37-38). The primitive community — which praised God or rejoiced in the sympathy of all the people — was a genuine, evangelical body which lived in the unity of the word of the apostles and the breaking of the bread, in common prayer and generous service to the brethren. "Breaking bread in their homes, they partook of food with glad and generous hearts" (Acts 2:42-47).

1. *Change as repentance*

In a genuine process of renewal the first step is repentance, that is, a change of mind and heart. "Repent and believe in the gospel" (Mk 1:15). "Be renewed in the spirit of your minds, and put on the new nature" (Eph 4:23).

If we have understood things superficially, we may have thrown ourselves precipitously into a mere modification of forms — changes in habit and office, external organisation of houses and opening to the public, planned suppression of works in order to make new experiments — but our hearts have not been touched and we have not conformed them thoroughly to Jesus Christ, nor have we accepted the demands of the gospel.

We need to ask ourselves whether our institutes are faithful to their "authentic and integral vocation" (ET 51), "to the mode of procedure which the call of God requires of spiritual families, with eyes wide open to the needs of society and its problems, and with that zest for the absolute which is the fruit of a sure experience of God" (ET 52).

The criterion of renewal is as follows: "I appeal to you therefore, brethren, by the mercies of God, to present your bodies as a living sacrifice, holy and acceptable to God, which is your spiritual worship. Do not be conformed to this world but be transformed by the renewal of your mind, that you may prove what is the will of God, what is good and acceptable and perfect" (Rom 12:1-2). Repentance demands poverty and humility: a clear consciousness of our own limits and wretchedness, a hunger for God and a need for the brethren. When we feel ourselves too secure — masters of truth and holiness, excessively sure of our loyalty to the charism of our Founder or to the requirements of the Spirit at this moment in the church's history — it is impossible really to practise fellowship. It is in fact difficult to divest ourselves of our own affairs so as to seek together, with absolute simplicity and disposability, the things of the Spirit.

Fortunately, in the present renewal of the religious life, there is a positive sign; poverty is favoured, the word of God is meditated on in community, the ways of the Spirit are sought in prayer, and there is an effort to die to self. Radical following of Christ in the religious life demands a continual process of repentance. We need every day to strip ourselves of "the old human nature", "to be renewed in the spirit of our minds" and "to put on the new nature", made after the likness of God in righteousness and true holiness (Eph 4:22-24).

Repentance — a sincere return to the Father and to our brother and sister in perfect love — is the work of every day; but there are moments in history when the call of the Spirit to repentance is of special urgency. Today we are living in the church through one of those privileged moments. "The time has arrived for hoping with the greatest seriousness for a rectification of our consciences, if that is necessary, and also for a revision of your whole lives in the direction of a greater loyalty" (ET 53).

When we speak of the renewal of the religious life, we mean to emphasise particularly three things:

— *"Newness in Christ"*, which is essentially the inner life, fulfilment and completion. "Think not that I have come to abolish the law and the prophets: I have not come to abolish them but to fulfil them" (Mt 5:17). The new is not simply the present and what has never been seen. The new is returning to the original freshness of the gospel — "the supreme and ultimate norm of the religious life" (PC 2) — discovering again the charism of our foundation and making it new in this juncture of the church and the world.

— *"Conversion of the heart"* is an indispensable condition for paschal renewal. "A new heart I will give you, and a new spirit I will put within you; and I will take out of your flesh the heart of stone and give you a heart of flesh" (Ezek 36:26). It is not just a matter of breaking with the past and adapting oneself superficially to a transient world (1 Jn 2:17): it is essentially a matter of understanding the "times and seasons" (Acts 1:7) in which God asks of us the perfection of charity, and humankind awaits the joy of salvation.

— *"Loyalty to the present requirements of the Spirit"*, who is leading us to live in contemplation and service, in "genuine love" (Rom 12:9), in seeking justice and practising peace.

2.   Testimony of the community

As a rule young people are attracted by people of strong personality, by genuine examples who live simply and joyfully, following their vocation with sincerity and unforced heroism. Therefore they feel disillusioned when they come across comfortable, mediocre communities, as they also feel disappointed by communities superficially "reformed" but not deeply converted and renewed in the

Spirit. So, the renewal of the religious life must result in the formation of poor, praying, fraternal and missionary communities. That is the best testimony for the evangelisation of the contemporary world. They must be communities which live in genuine love, firmly incorporated in Christ and open to the needs and aspirations of humankind; communities, big or little, which live in detachment and poverty deeply in prayer, true evangelical fraternity, and generous apostolic and missionary endeavour; communities which are witnesses to the saving presence of Jesus. They must be communities living in a profound consciousness of God and a serene sharing in the pain of the brethren, open and near to the people of our time, but still more, palpably indwelt by the Spirit, who is the Spirit of the inner life and prophecy, of fraternal fellowship and service, of joy in the cross and of mission.

Today the young lay great importance on the community aspect, but they want the community to be a genuine fellowship of people matured in Christ through faith, spurred on through hope and generously open to the world through charity. They want communities carrying out in their lives the gospel demands of St Paul: "We beseech you, brethren, to respect those who labour among you and are over you in the Lord and admonish you … . Be at peace among yourselves … . Rejoice always, pray constantly, give thanks in all circumstances; for this is the will of God in Christ Jesus for you. Do not quench the Spirit" (1 Thess 5:12-19).

3. Proclamation of the kingdom

Every religious life is a proclamation of the kingdom. Therefore, religious "have in their consecrated lives a special opportunity of effective evangelisation in the contemporary world" (EN 69). But they must proclaim by word and testify with their lives that the kingdom of God has already come, and that it is necessary to repent and accept the Good News.

The religious life, if it is lived authentically in the Spirit, is always a prophetic proclamation, a manifestation of the coming of the kingdom, a sign of God's holiness and an anticipation of eternal life. Thus it is always a proclamation of the "good news" of Jesus and a pressing invitation to hope. In this also the young feel a particular attraction towards the religious life. They feel, on the one hand, the force of Jesus' command: "Go into all the world and preach the gospel to the whole creation" (Mk 16:15). They feel with St Paul that to proclaim the Gospel is "a necessity laid upon" them. "Woe to me if I do not preach the gospel" (1 Cor 9:16). On the other hand, they see, and are in contact with, the wretchedness of humankind. They share the experience of the pain; they have a special sensitivity to hunger and injustice; they feel the need of being really poor; and in their hearts they feel a very strong call to "preach the good news to the poor ... to proclaim release to the captives and the recovering of sight to the blind, to set at liberty those that are oppressed" (Lk 4:18).

The religious life is an explicit proclamation of God's kingdom of justice, love and peace and, because of this, a concrete impulse for the liberation of humankind. Evangelisation and liberation have the same aim, complete salvation in Jesus Christ (cf. EN ch. 3). The young want to proclaim Christ "our blessed hope" (Tit 2:13); they want to play their part in the history of men and women by taking to them the "joy of salvation".

III. **The joy of hope**

"Let hope be genuine ... rejoice in your hope, be patient in tribulation, be constant in prayer" (Rom 12:9-12). As it is an urge deeply committed to the kingdom, the religious life is essentially a prophetic proclamation of hope and a simple communication of paschal joy. It is every day an experience of the resurrection of

Jesus. Young people are attracted by a deep and austere life, lived in the overflowing joy of fraternal fellowship and devoted in the service of hope for humankind.

Perhaps it is precisely this that is most convincing to the rising generations: communicating joy and generating hope in men and women. St Paul sees everything in a context of charity: "Let love be genuine ... rejoice in your hope, be patient in tribulation, be constant in prayer" (Rom 12:9-12). There is the joy of sincere love, of fulfilled hope, of continual prayer. It is the joy of total dedication to the kingdom, the joy of the "babes" to whom the Father reveals secrets hidden from the wise and prudent (Lk 10:21), the joy of the poor and patient, of those who suffer and hunger for righteousness, of the merciful and pure in heart, and of those who work for peace and are persecuted for righteousness' sake (Mt 5:3-10). It is the deep happiness of the kingdom, reserved for souls who have generously pledged their lives in absolute loyalty to the Word (Lk 1:45; 11:27) and whose existence is a "priceless testimony to the fact that the world cannot be transformed or offered to God except in the spirit of the beatitudes" (LG 31). Those who possess the kingdom and are its witnesses, are happy because they possess God whom they show and communicate to their fellow creatures. But it is only the poor and pure in heart, those who are living face to face with God and the brethren, who are nourished by contemplation and the cross, only they can enjoy this happiness and pass it on. Because of it, profound souls — those who, like Mary, live silently at the foot of the Cross — are imperturbably serene and able to communicate a deep, balanced and infectious joy. It is, ultimately, the joy of salvation, which is announced in the coming of the kingdom to Mary: "Hail, full of grace, the Lord is with you" (Lk 1:28). The gospel, being the Good News of salvation, is a call to joy: "I bring you good news of a great joy which will come to all the people; for to you is born this day in the city of David a Saviour, who is Christ the Lord" (Lk 2:10-11).

The religious life is, in fact, a prophetic witness of salvation and a radical dedication to the gospel; therefore, it is a proclamation and communication of joy on condition, we repeat, that it is lived in the depth of silence and the serene fruitfulness of the cross.

At times the paschal witness of Jesus' resurrection is missing in the consecrated life. Anxious enquiry is made about what the religious life really is. It is a way of expressing the anguish of the women at the sepulchre: "They have taken the Lord out of the tomb, and we do not know where they have laid him" (Jn 20:20) or the pessimism and grief of the Emmaus disciples: "We had hoped he was the one to redeem Israel" (Lk 24:21). In communities there often exists a void: that of the risen Christ. The joyful experience of the Spirit of love is also absent. It might be said that the religious life has not yet succeeded in instilling a very great consciousness of the adoption of sons, of universal brotherhood, and of the transforming presence of the Christ of Easter. "We have lost the Lord".

In some cases, to replace the lacking "Christ crucified", we have been to drink at "broken cisterns" (Jer 2:13); and so, very soon, bitterness has grown up, and with it bewilderment and discouragement; many vocations have been lost because the joy of the cross and the hope of the risen Lord have been lost. Either our consecrated life is an experience and witness of the fact that "we have found the Messiah ... the Christ" (Jn 1:41), or instead we are "of all men most to be pitied" (1 Cor 15:19).

A community which deeply lives the life of Christ who has annihilated himself — a poor, crucified Christ, a Christ praying and glorifying the Father is a community which irradiates the unconquerable joy of Easter, and a sign of credibility, a witness in fact of the clear and transforming presence of Christ, the Son of God and Lord of history, and of the life-giving action of the Holy Spirit who is the Spirit of fellowship. The most convincing sign of a genuine community which lives in sincere love and deep prayer is joy. Joy is an inner fruit of charity. The more intense the sacrifice to the Father is in religious consecration — the more definite the following of Christ is — and the truer and simpler dedication to the service of the brethren is, so much the more is the joy of Easter revealed and communicated in a community. The joy of the consecrated life again implies two things: being certain of God's faithfulness and a clear consciousness of one's own nature.

If we do not know what we are in the church — if we lose our specific character so as to confuse ourselves and regret that we have not other gifts and missions — we shall live in anguish and grief. We shall have lost the irreplaceable joy of what is ours (perhaps the joy in simple things of the child who offers his ingenuousness to disarm the worry and sorrow of grown-ups). We look for means of self-fulfilment by ways which are not specifically and providentially our own; and then, we shall never be happy. In fact our way of fulfilling ourselves, as Christians and as religious, is our decisive choice of Jesus Christ crucified. And this is the only language of salvation which the world expects of religious, today also, and perhaps principally today, even if, sometimes, we have the impression that it may also be "a stumbling-block and a folly" (1 Cor 1:18-25) for us.

We must savour in our hearts, very deeply, God's faithfulness to his promises. "He who calls you is faithful, and he will do it" (1 Thess 5:24). It is possible for our hearts to be sorrowful because of something we have desired and never achieved, because it is not God's will for us, or at least, not then. We can let ourselves be overcome by pessimism because of a change for which we are kept waiting, for a renewal in the community or institute which seems to us urgent but which we see is humanly unattainable. We can feel pain and sadness at absurd division in the congregation or at an almost massive exodus of young and capable members. We can also feel the hunger and wretchedness, the abandonment and pushing aside, the injustice and loneliness of so many of our

112

suffering brothers and sisters. How many motives there are for cutting off joy and quenching the power of hope!

However, today more than ever, if we mean to be faithful disciples of the kingdom and true servants of our fellow creatures, we must patiently embrace the cross and from it — from its wisdom and strength — make a beginning of our paschal witness of joy and hope which humankind has the right to demand of us, for Christ is risen and we have the obligation of proclaiming his kingdom of righteousness, holiness and grace, love and peace. Our cry must be this: "We have seen the Lord and he has said these things to us" (cf. Jn 20:18). "The Lord has risen indeed and has appeared to Simon" (Lk 24:34).

To sum up briefly, the joy of the religious life is the joy of a vivid experience of God aiming to make himself heard by the brethren. It is the joy of the Spirit (Gal 5:22) introducing us deeply into the truth of Christ (Jn 16:13), making us enjoy in prayer the silent meeting with the Father "who is in secret" (Mt 6:6) and giving us the joy of suffering (Col 1:24) and the exclusive glory of the cross (Gal 6:14). It is the joy of receiving the word even "in much affliction, with joy inspired by the Holy Spirit" (1 Thess 1:7) and announcing it to our fellow creatures by the witness of a life like "a letter from Christ delivered by us, written not with ink but with the spirit of the living God, not on tablets of stone but on the tablets of human hearts" (2 Cor 3:3). It is the joy of "perfect charity" which makes us exclusively "alive to God in Christ Jesus" (Rom 6:11) and in his humble attitude of service to the point of giving up his life for the brethren (Jn 15:12). It is the joy of a love made as an offering and gift in the consecrated life, and of the Spirit who dwells in us through contemplation, clothes us with his power for prophetic witness and drives us with his fiery energy for the apostolic mission.

It remains to say something more explicitly and concretely about the paschal hope as a requirement and sign

113

of the renewal of a religious life in the Spirit. Every consecrated life — every religious community — is a prophetic cry of hope. This is more necessary than ever in the confused and divided world in which we live. A life exclusively and radically dedicated to the gospel cannot help proclaiming that salvation has arrived, that the kingdom of God is henceforth in our midst, that Jesus is risen and is the Lord of history, and that we live in expectation of "our blessed hope, the appearing of our great God and Saviour Jesus Christ" (Tit 2:13).

If there is, in the process of renewal of the religious life, one thing which we must keep in mind and shout to the world, it is hope. This is an indispensable meeting-point with the rising generations. Formerly, the young simply thought about the future, now they prepare for it and bring it to life already, in the present. Therefore, the present — from the viewpoint of the church in general and the religious life in particular — must be laden with the fertility of hope.

What do we mean by "hope" when we are speaking of renewal of the religious life? Today, in fact, the young do not put up with passively waiting in a community which merely looks forward to the "Lord's coming". This is essentially here and now: "The Lord is at hand" (1 Cor 16:22). The cry, full of hope, of the christian community is: "Come, Lord Jesus!". It is also the deep and sorrowful hope of the whole creation, liberated in hope, which anxiously awaits the manifestation of God's glory in the redemption of our bodies, in the perfect fullness of our adoption as sons (Rom 8:19-24). This, however, is not enough: hope is something more: and the young expect something much fuller and more dynamic. The religious life must express clearly these three aspects of christian hope: the search for the ultimate (eschatological tension), daily involvement with history, and the certainty that Christ is risen.

A religious life is always a proclamation and a prophecy: a proclamation of the kingdom already begun

114

and an anticipation of the kingdom in its perfect state. Therefore, the religious life — in the sum total of its acts and words, in personal existence and in community life — must announce and proclaim eternal life. It must put the meaning and desire of the eternal into the hearts of peoples and nations. "Here we have no lasting city, but we seek the city which is to come" (Heb 13:14).

In the personal being of religious and in the manner of life of their communities, there is something which is a strong call to the ultimate. Also, in teaching human beings to love life, to transform the world and bring history into being, the religious life is essentially a call to the inner life and transcendence: "If you then have been raised with Christ, seek things that are above, where Christ is, seated at the right hand of God. Set your minds on things that are above, not on things that are on earth. For you have died, and your life is hid with Christ in God. When Christ who is our life appears, then you also will appear with him in glory" (Col 3:1-4).

Communities genuinely renewed, so that they understand deeply the mystery of the human species and his history, anticipate the perfect kingdom and proclaim prophetically "new heavens and a new earth in which righteousness dwells" (2 Pet 3:13). But christian hope is essentially active and creative and assumes in religious, principally in them, a firm commitment to history. For them, too, the words of the Council are valid: "Eschatological hope does not diminish the importance of earthly efforts, but also gives new reasons for continuing to undertake them" (GS 21).

Here arises the problem of social, economic and political effort by religious, that is the problem of their taking a place in history, of their active participation in changing the world and creating a new society, and of their solidarity with those who suffer and struggle, die and hope. Only in the heart of christian hope, understood as the dynamism of a faith which overflows in charity, is it possible rightly to set the efforts of religious and their evangelical presence in the world. They will continue to be witnesses to God's absolute reality, signs of his holiness and prophets of the kingdom in its perfection. It will be necessary to avoid two extremes: running away from history and merely identifying themselves with the world.

How are they to share fully the lot of their fellow human beings — the life of the poor — without losing the "originality" of Christianity or the "specificity" of the religious life? It is only possible to achieve it by starting from the heart of a hope which, on the one hand makes human beings mobile, and, on the other, commands them to cultivate the earth. In other words, this hope reminds them that "our commonwealth is in heaven, and from it we await a Saviour, the Lord Jesus Christ" (Phil 3:20), but at the same time, forbids them merely to "stand looking up into heaven" (Acts 1:11) and commands them to "go into all the world and preach to all men the Good News of salvation" (Mk 16:15).

The religious life cannot stand aloof from human history for it is an active part of that history itself. Further, it has to bring to history the transforming fruits of the Beatitudes of the gospel. But this means that its real membership in the world, and its true impact on the social, economic and political reality of society can only start from the complete inner experience of the paschal mystery, that is of the power of hope. Only those who have learnt to deny themselves wholly in Christ and to die are capable of properly serving their brethren and of rising again in them as though by a gift which gives life; only they can pass on to men and women liberty and peace, and establish them in righteousness. The total following of Christ in the religious life obliges people to "re-awaken their consciences with regard to the drama of wretchedness and the demands for social justice of the gospel and the church" (ET 18). Because of this, hope must be an absolute certainty of the presence of the risen Christ. Believing in Jesus' resurrection is not just celebrating a life-giving event: it is, above all, knowing

116

by experience that Christ is alive and continues to accompany us, and that he is the Lord of history.

In this sense, the religious life is the powerful affirmation of Jesus' coming and presence, of the life-giving action of the Holy Spirit in the progressive building up of the kingdom which is to be consigned to the Father, and of the security given by knowing that we are a people which walks unflinchingly "among the persecutions of the world and the consolations of God, proclaiming the Lord's cross until he comes" (LG 8).

Hope is, therefore, trust in God "for whom nothing is impossible" (Lk 1:27; Jn 18:14). It is infallible confidence "in the love of God, in Christ Jesus our Lord" (Rom 8:39). It is, ultimately, an act of faith in the trustworthiness of the Father, in the redemptive work of the Son and the sanctifying gift of the Holy Spirit.

Conclusion

Renewal of the religious life — expected by all, promised by the church and required by the Spirit — always comes in the paschal newness of life, coming from progressive incorporation in the death and resurrection of the Lord (Rom 6:4). It involves a continuous process of conversion; it requires one to enter deeply into the life of the cross and contemplation, to pay attention to new calls from the Lord every day, to be generously faithful to his word, to form praying, fraternal and missionary communities, to serve one's fellows by sharing their sufferings, and to express oneself in the Lord in the simplicity and joy which sound a cry of hope to the whole world. All this means building together the paschal church, the church of the kenosis, the church of poverty and service, of contemplation and the word, of the cross and of hope, of fellowship and of mission, the church which is a sacrament of the paschal Christ: "Christ in you, the hope of glory" (Col 1:27).

In the heart of this paschal church, we live the life which is the gift of the Spirit in the religious life. Today, more than ever, we experience the joy of his presence and the fruitfulness of his mission. The young look on with hope; they want something new which may interpret to them their hunger for total sacrifice, for a genuine life of fellowship, for profound contemplation, and for sincere, simple and joyful giving. In these ways — the ways of the Spirit which are the true ways of the paschal Christ — the authentic renewal of the religious life must progress. Let us painfully seek its pattern. Perhaps we shall find it, if we are humbler and more sincere, if we pray more and with greater faith, if we lay ourselves open to the Father and the brethren with a greater hunger for truth and less confidence in our own capabilities.

May our Mother Mary, the lowly handmaid of the Lord, make us all faithful and blessed (Lk 1:45); may she teach us the joy of contemplation (Lk 2:19-51) and the power of the cross (Jn 19:25). May she prepare us in prayer and fellowship for the missionary dynamism of the Spirit (Acts 1:14). May she sing to the Father the song of the poor in us: "My spirit rejoices in God my Saviour, for he has regarded the low estate of his handmaiden" (Lk 1:47-48). Yet, above all, may Mary open to consecrated souls the way of Easter renewal, may she pass on to them the deep joy of loyalty to the Father (Lk 1:48), and teach them that there is no other way of satisfying the hope of the young, of changing history and of bringing together everything in Christ, than that of listening to her words: "Do whatever he tells you" (Jn 2:5). Without doubt, this is to be the hope of the young. There was in fact, a young woman, who in the fullness of time, felt the yearnings of the people and the love of the Father, believed in him and dedicated herself to his plan of salvation. Her faithfulness changed history. Therefore, she is the "cause of our joy" and "the mother of holy hope". "Her name was Mary" (Lk 1:27).

REFECTIONS FOR A CHAPTER MEETING

I HAVE BEEN THINKING before God of what a Chapter meeting means in the church. And the first thing that came to my mind was that a chapter is of primary importance to the church and to the world. This means that it is not merely the question of an act of habit, more or less important according to the matters raised, even though it be undertaken within the private life of a congregation or an institute.

In the first place, a chapter meeting is of concern to the whole church (it is an act of the church, even if the congregation is small and does not cover the whole world). Consequently, it is of concern to everyone (it is an event with a bearing on salvation, even if most people do not really know how to explain what a chapter really is). Because of this, I have decided to pen these thoughts. I would not like to think in fact that a chapter is of concern to its delegates only (or simply to the members of the institute only). I am sorry to have to point out that, for the most part, chapters are held without anyone — in the church or in the world — going so far as to take any interest in them, whereas in fact every chapter ought to be a new and deeper manifestation of God to those in the church. That is a "genuine event", a page of hope. I do not intend to create a "chapter theology", much less to give rules or practical directions. I merely would like to offer these simple pastoral reflections, born of a deep love for the church, in order to emphasise some aspects which seem to me essential.

A chapter is always a "paschal celebration". To that end, it must be framed in an essential context of Easter, with all that which Easter contains with regard to the cross and hope, to death and resurrection. A chapter is essentially a paschal celebration. It is therefore, first of all, a "penitential" celebration, which involves a strong commitment to two things: a sincere attitude of repentance, and a deep and painful search for the paths of the Lord. God's ways need to be discovered every day in pain and hope. Just because a chapter is a penitential celebration, it is always carried out in the joy and sincerity of fraternal love. How important it is to emphasise the penitential aspect of a chapter! That means a sincere and profound examination of conscience, with the consequent change of mind and life; it means a painful search for the will of God in the present demands of the religious life. How are we to practise and deepen our incorporation in the Christ of Easter by means of the consecrated life's confirmation of baptism? What are we to do to make the consecrated life today truly a sign of the holiness of God and the presence of his kingdom?

But, because it is a genuine paschal celebration, it is not only the penitential aspect which interests us in a chapter. It is the whole dimension of paschal newness of life — of new creation in the Spirit — and of creative hope therein which is of essential importance. Every chapter should leave behind a sense of freshness in the church, a good measure of Easter optimism. If the chapter has been well celebrated, in an attitude of poverty, prayer and fraternal love, it is always a re-creation of the institute, which allows its spiritual wealth to overflow onto the church and the world. Because of all this, the chapter is a saving event, an ecclesial act and a family happening.

I. A saving event

God works in history without ceasing. After Christ came into the world, in the fullness of time, he does not cease to reconcile men and women and things with the

Father. Christ, exalted at the right hand of the Father, and constituted Lord of the universe, daily sends his Spirit over the whole universe and makes him dwell in the heart of each person who is called to share in the paschal mystery of Christ (GS 22).

There are, however, key moments in the story of salvation: e.g., the call of Abram, the release of the people from slavery in Egypt and that people's wandering in the wilderness, the entry into the promised land, the return from the Babylonian exile, the redemptive incarnation of Jesus, with his Easter consummated in Pentecost. When, with the outpouring of the Holy Spirit, the stage of the maturity of hope began, key events were to take place, marking themselves out by the production of the fruits of salvation. Such, for example, are the celebration of a Council, the election of a Pope, or a religious persecution. In this connection, the second Vatican Council was a saving event for our own times (deplorably, as often happens, we have not drawn sufficient profit from it).

It is in this sequence — though, naturally at a very, very great distance and in an extremely modest and simple setting — that I place a chapter. It constitutes a moment of our Lord's particular presence and a pouring out of the Spirit, not only in the particular community but throughout the whole church. And, since the church is essentially a universal sacrament of salvation (LG 48; GS 45), it is the whole world which feels the great benefits of a chapter. With the internal renewal of an institute — wrought in depth, balance and boldness of the Spirit — the church is spiritually enriched, and the world receives its fruits.

The holding of a chapter is a great moment in the story of salvation which an institute must write, "not with ink but with the Spirit of the living God, not on tablets of stone but on tablets of human hearts" (2 Cor 3:3). However, for a chapter really to be a saving event, three things must enter into it: the word, the Holy Spirit, repentance.

1. Repentance

It is from here that salvation starts. The Good News, proclaimed to the poor, is for the salvation of all those who believe (Rom 1:16) and, for this, repentance and faith are necessary (Mk 1:15). A chapter is always, by the power of the gospel, a call to repentance. The first to assume the responsibility, representing all the brethren, are the members of the chapter themselves. So, the first necessity in electing a member of chapter is not his intelligence, but his elementary capacity for repentance. A chapter is measured not by the depth and elegance of its documents, but rather by its capability of transforming the minds and hearts of all. Is all this difficult? Humanly speaking, yes. But two other elements are still needed: the word and the Spirit.

2. The Word

A chapter is, above all, a means of "hearing the word of God and keeping it" (Lk 11:28). But it is necessary to hear it together, so as to be able to put it into practice in common. The president of a chapter must always be the Word of God, that is, Christ. Then the chapter will turn out to be irresistible. During the Council the book of the gospel was enthroned every day before the sessions were declared open. It was a most solemn rite. Would it not be expedient to do the same in chapters, since it is God who is to speak in them? He does this primarily through holy scripture, the Magisterium of the church, and the spirit and charism of the Founders. But he does it also through the requirements of new ages in the church, the events of history and sincere discussion with the brethren.

That implies that all, privately and together, set themselves humbly to meditate on the word of God. The central moments of a chapter are, then, great moments of prayer. Otherwise human words are multiplied uselessly and tensions grow. Maybe, wonderful decrees and directions result from them, but minds and hearts will remain unchanged.

3. *The Holy Spirit*

The great event of salvation — the mystery of the redemptive incarnation culminating in Pentecost — was wrought by virtue of the fruitful action of the Holy Spirit. So it must be now also. The paschal renewal of a chapter does not exist without the creative power of the Holy Spirit. We must allow ourselves to be led by him. It is he who makes us aware of the Lord's passage in history, who deciphers and interprets the signs of the times and who calls us to genuine change in repentance. A chapter is always fundamentally a work of the Holy Spirit. It is not made up of geniuses, but of ordinary persons with the ability to be inspired by the Spirit. The Spirit of Truth is the testimony of endurance and martyrdom, of the contemplative inner life and of prophecy.

II. An ecclesial act

A chapter is not the private affair of a congregation or an institute; but essentially an ecclesial act. It is so for two reasons: the whole ecclesial community has something to say in a chapter (it takes part actively, even if not immediately present), and the whole ecclesial community draws benefit from the fruits in the chapter. Consequently it is absurd to hold a chapter without taking into account the actual state of the church. The first question in a chapter is always this: what does the world expect of us today? All institutes were born to meet a definite need of the church in a particular period of history.

There was a period, immediately after the Council, during which congregations held special chapters of "aggiornamento", they tried to interpret the church and to "fall into line". They succeeded in part; but in part, no; either because they went too far, or because they were excessively timid; either because they stopped at "external conformity" only, or because they took risks with their original charism and changed it.

When, therefore, we say that a chapter is an ecclesial act it is our intention to mean three things: that the chapter must look to Christ, that it must keep in touch with the world, and that it must integrate itself in the local christian community.

1. *Looking to Christ*

The church is, before all, the sacrament of the paschal Christ, in other words, a sign and instrument of the saving presence of Jesus. So, a chapter aims at the renewal of the institute by a progressive conformation with Christ. It is fundamentally an answer to the following question: How much do our community or members and institutions show forth and communicate the Lord? Therefore, a chapter always confronts the institutions with the people's expectations: "We wish to see Jesus" (Jn 12:21). The first call to it is made by Christ who was sent by the Father "not to condemn the world but that the world might be saved through him" (Jn 3:17). His fundamental question is this: "Who do men say that I am?" (Mt 16:15).

2. *The world*

Every chapter belongs to a given moment in history; it must interpret and respond evangelically to men and women who are waiting for salvation. The church offers itself to them as a sign and instrument of the complete salvation brought to them by Christ the Lord. Therefore, a chapter — which is always looking for the Lord in the desert through the transforming action of the Spirit — is placed at the same time in close relation with the world. It is bound to see the growing expectation of nations and the anxiety and hope of humankind in the signs of the times. And since it is an ecclesial event, the chapter cannot be confined to reviewing the problems of one congregation only. It must be essentially an evangelical reflection on the needs and aspirations of the church at that particular time. It must ask itself, for instance, what evangelisation means in the church today, who are the poor today, what meaning have education, social assistance, human progress, the full liberation of nations.

3. *The local christian community*

All religious life is a part of a definite christian community. It draws its substance therefrom, grows within it and animates it. Therefore, the individual church (or a local community) has much interest in a chapter. In some way its aspirations and its talents must reach the chapter. During the holding of the chapter the whole individual church takes an interest in it and prays for it. It is a privileged time for the life of that church: there is also a special outpouring of the Holy Spirit over it, with a strong call to repentance. The life of an institute does not grow "alongside" the local community, but "within" it; it is nourished by the same word and by the Eucharist, it is brought together by the Holy Spirit in the same centre of unity, which is the bishop "who is assisted by the elders" (LG 21). So a bishop, with his clergy and his people, is not a stranger or observer at the chapter. He is there because something of great importance to the church is happening. So, above all, the personal meeting with the Pope, when it is possible, is not merely an act of devotion, but the affirmation that the chapter is above all an act of ecclesial fellowship.

III. A family event

Every chapter is a family gathering; its centre is Jesus. "The apostles returned to Jesus" (Mk 6:30). Therefore,

125

again, the word and the action of the Holy Spirit are central to this gathering. The members of an institute come together to pray, to receive the word of God in common, to take cognizance of the activities and demands of the Spirit, to renew the joy of perseverance in the consecrated life and look again at their own charism, to hear together a new call to repentance and to commit themselves more forcefully in the evangelisation of the contemporary world; in other words, to think more deeply of the mystery of the church and, with it, of the specific demands of its religious consecration and the ever new meaning of the charism of its foundation.

This family gathering needs to be undertaken in an atmosphere of extraordinary poverty, of continual prayer and of great fraternal love. In such a way, useless tension, confusion, ambiguity, and superficial misunderstandings will be avoided. The atmosphere of a chapter appears at once in "glad and generous hearts" (Acts 2:46). The sincerity, balance and effectiveness of a chapter depend on its depth of prayer. Then, indeed, a chapter is truly a paschal celebration.

This, however, requires a spirit of true *evangelical poverty*. The first condition for being a member of a chapter is to be really poor. Thus he will be a "God-hearer". So also he will be a person open to "dialogue". Any one who goes into a chapter sure that he knows everything (that he has a monopoly of real truth) can never lay himself open to the fruitful action of the Spirit of truth whom Jesus promised us (Jn 16:13), nor to be available to others with simplicity. And the others, for their part, will not be able to open out to him. Poverty opens us to God in prayer, for the chapter member feels the responsibility of his mission — which is not his since it has been entrusted to him in the institute and, fundamentally in the church — therefore he feels the need to pray.

A chapter always implies a great atmosphere of *evangelical freedom*. Every one ought, in loyalty to the

Spirit who speaks within him, to be able to show his own opinion freely and to receive the opinions of others gladly. The chapter must really be a fertile debate in the Spirit; fundamentally, it is born of a common experience of poverty, of the knowledge of the same responsibility and of the same attitude of "listening to the word of God". No one in the church is in possession of complete truth. Therefore the poor who, void of self, are exclusively open to the Holy Spirit, have much to say and contribute to a chapter.

Another essential element in this family event is *prayer*. We have already remarked that the chapter must be a meeting with the Lord, a true paschal celebration whose centre is the Eucharist. The institute's life must be thoroughly revised in the light of God's word. It is this which makes us see things clearly, it is this above all which calls us to repentance.

Finally, the family meeting of a chapter demands a joyful and simple atmosphere of fraternal love. This makes freedom in debate easy. The members' living together in the Spirit must be a testimony for the other members of the institute. By this I do not mean to say that differences of opinion will not exist (that is an indispensable quality of a genuine fellowship which is the fruit of the pluriform action of the Holy Spirit), but everything must be carried out with great mutual respect, not with the aggressiveness and self-satisfaction of those who feel they are masters of absolute truth, but with the humility of those who have much to receive and feel themselves as tools of the Holy Spirit.

This quality of fraternal love must not remain shut up in the immediate circle of a chapter. It is to spread to all the members of the institute, whom the capitulars must interpret, bear in mind and serve. For this reason again, the chapter does not need to have geniuses; it needs to have the poor, those persons capable of being possessed by the Holy Spirit, with great docility towards him and with a great spirit of understanding and service. That is to say, it needs men and women who will live "according to the Spirit" and are ready to die to themselves or renounce their own ideas, so that Christ may grow in the world and that the Father may be glorified. Sincere men or women who are trying to love God and listen to the brethren are what is wanted.

But there is something else. This line of fraternal love leads us to think of the concrete situation of an individual church (or of the universal church) and in the general expectation of the world. In fact, a chapter is always a way of entering into saving fellowship with the whole people of God and with the generality of peoples on pilgrimage towards the Father. Let us return to the basic idea we began with: a chapter is not a private affair of the capitulars or the members of an institute. It is primarily an affair of the church, which is of concern to everyone and to all peoples.

Therefore a chapter cannot be held without preparation, nor can it be celebrated as if it were in hiding. It must be known by all, accompanied by all with prayer and the cross, celebrated by all with the responsibility of repentance, and welcomed by all with hope. A chapter is always a work of the love of God, "poured into our hearts through the Holy Spirit who has been given to us" (Rom 5:5). Therefore it is a new and wonderful passage in the history of salvation. Let us all celebrate it with gratitude and readiness for God's service, like Mary, the lowly handmaid of the Lord, in whom God worked wonders and through whom "the day which shall dawn on us from on high" (Lk 1:78) shone throughout the whole world.

ON THE SINCERITY OF LOVE
Points for a priestly spirituality

> Let love be genuine (Rom 12:9).
>
> Rejoice in your hope, be patient in tribulation, be constant in prayer (Rom 12:12).

Introduction

TIME passes so quickly — and cultural, social and political changes cut so deeply into the lives and missions of priests — that we have not a moment to spare on the simple description of what a priest ought to be today. We need to anticipate time and penetrate into the future with the luminous audacity of a prophet. Today he who trains priests must be specially inspired by the spirit of prophecy. So he must be a man of prayer, thoroughly poor and very realistic.

What I can say to you is no more than the fruit of love and experience. The Lord allowed me the grace, from the very first day of my ordination to the priesthood, to work particularly with seminarists and priests. That is why I have always talked of the paschal joy of being a priest. He also gave me the grace of loving my priesthood intensely. For this reason I have also felt a special predilection for priests.

I would like to centre these brief reflections in the following words of St Paul: "Let love be genuine" (Rom 12:9) and in Jesus' prayer: "Father, sanctify them in the truth; thy word is truth" (Jn 17:17). I would also like the atmosphere of this conversation to be that of a simple Advent meditation: let us await together the coming of the Lord, together we will celebrate Christmas, now so near, and together preach the final coming of Jesus: "The Lord is at hand" (Phil 4:5) "Come, Lord Jesus".

What does living in genuine love mean? From the human point of view, the first thing I should look for in a priest is for him to be a man with an unusual capacity for loving; that he himself, in the daily testimony of his life, should be a continual expression of a God who is essentially love (1 Jn 4:7). We learn this above all when the Lord submits us to the inescapable discipline of suffering. I would say that the capacity for loving confers it and the capacity for the cross and death expresses it. "Greater love has no man than this, that a man lay down his life for his friends" (Jn 15:13).

The priestly life is understood only — in its essential ministry and in its practical requirements — in the basic character of love. It is a fruit of God's love for humankind. It is an expression of Christ's love: "As the Father has loved me, so have I loved you ... I have called you friends ... I chose you" (Jn 15:9-16).

The priestly life does not make sense if it is not lived in the joyful loyalty of love; loyalty to Jesus Christ in silence, in the cross, and in service; loyalty to his fellow creatures in the full understanding of their problems and in unselfish dedication to their integral salvation. "For us men and for our salvation". This basic character of love — which we translate in the terms of authentic "pastoral charity" — is what lights up the obligations of contemplation and of the cross, of the preaching of the word, of the celebration of the sacrament (whose centre is the Eucharist) and of the service of the brethren, of poverty, of consecrated chastity and of mature obedience in the faith. Now, St Paul speaks of "genuine love". That means three things:

— that we be truly *faithful to our vocation and mission;* i.e., that we do not cease to be what we essentially are and what the world requires and expects of us;

— that we live in the simplicity and clarity of *truth.* From the human point of view, and also from God's point of view, there is no more terrible thing than a priest who is not authentic, i.e., who uses human diplomacy and duplicity. It is dreadful when one has to unravel the meaning of a brother's words and acts, whether those who praise him are killing him, and those who seek him are making use of him;

— that we do not *put asunder what God has united;* it is worth saying that we live in unbreakable unity between the love of God and of our neighbour, between contemplation and action. They are distinct realities which are inseparably united.

The priestly life and ministry must be lived in "genuine love", which I would like to expound under the following three classic and simple headings: the priest as teacher of prayer, as principle of fellowship, and as prophet of hope.

I. The teacher of prayer

We are used to defining the priest as "the man of God", "Tu, autem, o homo Dei". This definition continues to be valid. He is the man who always speaks of God and from God, who shows and communicates God, who bears God. So he must be the man who speaks uninterruptedly with God "face to face, as a man speaks with his friend" (Ex 33:11). That is to say, he must be a "man of prayer".

However, the men and women of today — specially the rising generations — insist that the priest be further a "teacher of prayer", who instructs them in prayer. There is a genuine search for contemplation in the young people of today. A short while ago the true priestly leader was one who could organise an apostolic movement perfectly, or, in some cases, could encourage the young greatly in social and political enterprise. Today, the real leader is he who satisfies the hunger for prayer and teaches the

131

secrets of genuine prayer. "Lord, teach us to pray" (Lk 11:1).

Further, the priest must be *a prophet and a witness*. "I appointed you a prophet to the nations" (Jer 1:5). "You shall be my witnesses" (Sir 1:8). Yet prophecy and testimony imply a powerful experience of God in the solitude of the desert and the fruitfulness of contemplation. "That which we have seen and heard we proclaim also to you" (1 Jn 1:3). The priest is not just a professional theologian; he is the true sage who passes on, by the power of the Spirit, what he has enjoyed in contemplation: "sapiens est non solum discens sed et patiens divina" (St Thomas). It is clear that this experience of God — this delightful knowledge of divine reality "per connaturalitatem" — is not confined exclusively to peak moments of prayer, but it undoubtedly involves them.

Contemplation is a certain capability of finding God in the simplicity of the revealed word or in the active silence of the desert, as also in the events of history or in the face of every person who walks with us on our pilgrimage. A genuine contemplative possesses a strong intuition for recognising the passage of the Lord in history and for communicating his presence to others: "It is the Lord" (Jn 21:7). One of the responsibilities of the priest as a "teacher of prayer" is to give the young a taste for the fecundity of contemplation, its intimate relation with life and its immediate connection with action. It is the way of overcoming every sort of dualism: faith and life, God and one's neighbour, prayer and effort, church and world, time and eternity.

Contemplation is indispensable for a priest, not only for the effectiveness of his apostolic activity but also for the balance and maturity of his own personality. A deep communication with God in prayer makes the priest balanced and serene, joyful and helpful, open and sincere. It gives him a special joy and strength in the Holy Spirit for overcoming difficult moments and making him a permanent witness of Easter. It immerses him in loyalty to

God, and makes him available for service to the "word of truth". Prayer is a way of making us grow in our "genuine love", that is, in the generosity of our dedication to Christ and to persons, and in the simplicity, clarity and authenticity of all our actions. Contemplation helps us to be veracious, and prevents our being infected by complication and intrigue. A contemplative — who lives in an authentic experience of God in the faith — neither seeks anything nor looks for any reward. He is concerned only with the glory of God and service to his brethren. He loves by preference "life hidden with Christ in God" (Col 3:3), appreciates the feeling of "sincere love of the brethren" (1 Pet 1:22), knows how to "rejoice with those who rejoice, and weep with those who weep" (Rom 12:15) and expects from the Lord only the "crown of righteousness" reserved for "all who have loved his appearing" (2 Tim 4:8).

But the prayer itself must also be "veracious", that is, a genuine communication with God, and even more, a profound communion with the Father's adorable will. This involves a clear consciousness of our poverty and a joyful experience of the divine fatherhood: "Go into your room and shut the door and pray to your Father who is in secret" (Mt 6:6). A "veracious" prayer is always *biblical, liturgical and ecclesial*. The priest — a teacher of prayer — feeds on the word of God, celebrates it in the Eucharist, and puts it into practice daily in the heart of the church.

Nevertheless, so that it may be "veracious", and by the very requirement of the word of God "made flesh" (Jn 1:14), prayer is *realistic* and *definite*. On the one hand, it assumes the "joys and hopes, the pains and the anxieties of the men and women of our time" (GS 1), and, on the other — from the contemplative inner life — it helps to interpret "the signs of the times" and to discover the permanent presence of Jesus in history.

Preparing a priest for our time — and for the future — means preparing him to live in "genuine love". Therefore — as a first condition — he must be prepared to be a "teacher of prayer" and he must be trained to be a balanced, normal, simple and sincere man, with a strong capacity for calm contemplation.

II. A principle of fellowship

The priest finds his identity in a special conformation with Christ as Head. "The function of presbyters, in so far as they are closely bound up with the episcopal order, shares in the authority by which Christ himself develops, sanctifies and governs his own body. For this reason the priesthood of the presbyters, while presupposing the sacraments of christian initiation, has been conferred by that special sacrament by which presbyters, by virtue of the anointing of the Holy Spirit, are distinguished by a special character which so conforms them to Christ the priest that they can act in the person of Christ, the head of the church" (PO 2). This results in the priest being the principle of fellowship in the church. He is the man who, by the authority of Christ and as a symbol of the Holy Spirit — "principium unitatis in communione" (LG 13) — makes and presides over the fellowship. This is indicated essentially by the word which he proclaims and by the Eucharist which he celebrates.

From this arise many requirements for his priestly spirituality. He will have to be, primarily, a man who lives in communion with Jesus Christ in prayer, in the cross and in sincere charity, a man firmly led by the Holy Spirit towards the depth of the desert, towards the evangelisation of his brethren and towards the generous dedication of his life up to the death of the cross. He will have to be, in addition, a man who knows how to live in fellowship: with the bishop, with the other presbyters and with all the people of God. Obedience — responsible and willing — is a sort of living in fellowship (PO 15). Christ brought about unity when "he humbled himself and became obedient unto death, even death on a cross" (Phil 2:8). However it is no question of a formal cold obedience, much less of an obedience which is calculated by self-interest or fear, but rather of an obedience rooted in faith and genuine love. It is, therefore, a clear and generous, mature and responsible obedience. He must think of the bishop — notwithstanding his limitations and defects — as of Christ himself, and love him like a true father, brother and friend.

Priestly friendship is today one of the most strongly appreciated and desired of human virtues. No one should be ordained who is not capable of making true friends, beginning with the basic friendship with Christ: "You are my friends ..." (Jn 15:13-15), and then continuing with genuine friendship with the other presbyters with whom he lives deeply united "by an intimate sacramental brotherhood" (PO 8).

Yet priestly friendship demands renunciation and death, permanent spiritual nearness and a sincere pursuit of the good of one's friends. Only the really poor — who trust entirely in the Lord and have no ambition — are capable of making friends. A real priestly friendship is a gift from God; still more, it is a fundamental experience of divine friendship. It helps us to live with joy under the radical demands of our consecration and ministry. It throws light on the cross of obedience and the joyful fecundity of priestly celibacy. So everything places it in the essential dimension of genuine love: for God and for the brethren. There are moments in the life of a priest when priestly friendship is absolutely necessary: when there is much suffering or human triumph. A human triumph — particularly when it was neither desired nor sought — always results, ultimately, in a cross. One needs someone to be there to share the pain.

When we speak of the priest as the principle of fellowship we mean also something else; that he is the man who preaches and effects *reconciliation*. St Paul says that God entrusted to us "the ministry of reconciliation" and "the message of reconciliation" (2 Cor 5:18-19). This implies being the man of all and for all. He cannot make a choice which excludes or discriminates, even if his ministry will necessarily have to be included in a fixed historical context and his evangelical predilections will be for the really poor and needy.

Being a principle of fellowship implies *preaching the exacting love of God*, the urgency of repentance and the fruitfulness of peace, undergoing the violence of the kingdom, but constantly proclaiming to his fellows the necessity of being genuine "peacemakers", a peace which is certainly not easy because it must be built by all, from within, and is the fruit of genuine righteousness and sincere love. Reconciling — by word and sacrament — involves learning to die every day. Jesus Christ reconciled the world with the Father and human beings with each other by "the cross, thereby bringing the hostility to an end" (Eph 2:16). This he was to do in such a way that unity would not be transitory and apparent, the fruit of convenience or fear, but real fellowship with the Lord and true fruit of the Spirit.

Being a principle of fellowship is fundamentally allowing oneself to be flooded by the Spirit of God and deeply embedded in Christ, and to have a true sense of the church. In the training of priests these are indispensable and essential.

An authentic priestly spirituality must be strongly *ecclesial*. An authentic theology of the church — principally of a particular church, as a concrete and immediate way of realising the universal church — is basic in the training of priests, specially today.

To be a man of the church! This is an essential requirement in one who trains priests, a man who passionately loves the church because he has found Christ in her and knows that humankind is waiting for his presence. But we must get to grips with the problem. At times it seems that we are "churchmen" because it is much more comfortable for us to place ourselves within its framework. The church is essentially the "great sacrament"

— sign and communication — of Christ being constantly sent by the Father for the salvation of the world.

Consequently, loving and living in the mystery of the church is finding in her the continual presence of the Easter Christ (dead and risen), her nature of being the fellowship of all the people of God (the church as a "sacrament of unity", LG 1) and her fundamental missionary character as "universal sacrament of salvation" (LG 48; AG 1).

A real trainer of priests must have a sense of the permanent *"essentiality"* and *"reality"* of the church. He must help to discover, love and live in the essential mystery of the church in the present day.

I should like, therefore, to point out three needs in this training in the meaning of the church:

— the church is primarily a *permanent presence of Christ*, built on the foundation of the apostles and inwardly animated by the Spirit. It is the inseparable unity of institution and charism;

— the church comes to being in a stated *historical context* which must be discovered and realised. Each individual church has its own specific character and vocation. This is where the need for a priestly life to be lived in the fellowship of the people of God comes in;

— the church is constantly *sent into the world* to reconcile it with the Father: this is the meaning of incarnation and presence, of mission and evangelisation.

III.   A prophet of hope

A priest's life and ministry are essentially a proclamation and celebration of Easter, and so a clear and permanent witness of hope. The priest is a sign of "the goodness and loving-kindness of God our Saviour" (Tit 3:4). The strength of our hope is based on God's faithfulness. Perhaps, never so much as today, has it

137

been necessary to preach, and to live in, hope. We live
— even within the church — through moments of darkness and seeking, when the temptation to weariness,
pessimism and gloom comes easily. The priest cries, in the
name of the Lord, "Do not be afraid", "I am with you",
"I will be with you always".

When we speak of the priest as a "prophet of hope"
we are hinting at something deeper still. Above all, he is
the man — consecrated by the Spirit — who proclaims to
us the "mighty works of God" (Acts 2:11). A prophet
is primarily he who makes us enter with joy the invisible
things of God. It is because of this that the prophet is of
interest not merely in his words but principally in his
person; there are prophetic *beings* and there are prophetic
acts. He who lives, for example, in the constant serenity
of a real love — offered as a sacrifice to the Father and
as service to humankind — by his silence tells us *who*
God is: "God is love", "He who abides in love abides in
God, and God abides in him" (1 Jn 4:16). Because of this
the prophet is a continual call to repentance and belief in
the love of God.

The priest, since he proclaims the invisible things of
God and the final end of human beings, must bear witness
of them with the *holiness of his life*. Like Christ he will
have to be "the image of the invisible God" (Col 1:15).
This brings a particular identification with the death and
resurrection of Jesus Christ. More than any one else the
priest shares St Paul's deep christian and apostolic experience: "I have been crucified with Christ; it is no longer
I who live, but Christ who lives in me" (Gal 2:9-20).

The priest is a prophet of hope because he anticipates
and proclaims the definitive. In the letter to the Hebrews
the basic conduct of the priest — following Christ — is
leading his people to their ultimate rest in God. The priest
sows in the hearts of all persons the burning love of the
manifestation of the Lord; "Come, Lord Jesus". He does
not do it as an escape or because he is weary (as when
the prophet Elijah begs the Lord for death): "It is enough;

now, O Lord, take away my life" (1 Kg 19:4) but as the fullness of the joy of meeting. Meanwhile there is need to live the present moment intensely — loyalty to the mission, joy of the cross, care and service of the brethren — with the heart open to what is totally new and final.

Christian hope — in its basis, its demands and its ends — is magnificently summarised in St Paul's sentence which is read in the liturgy of the holy night at Christmas: "For the grace of God has appeared for the salvation of all men, training us to renounce irreligion and worldly passions, and to live sober, upright and godly lives in this world, awaiting our blessed hope, the appearing of our great God and Saviour Jesus Christ" (Tit 2:11-13).

Being a prophet of hope means unravelling the true meaning of history and firmly involving everyone in it. Hope is not a superficial announcement of easy things, but rather discovering the footstep of the Lord in difficulties. It is not avoiding — for comfort or through fear — present responsibility, but assuming calmly and competently the mission of building the kingdom of God in the human city. Being a prophet is not an easy thing; much less is being a prophet of hope. We must, like Abram, believe against all hope, and have experience of a God who loves us and asks the impossible. We must be poor, give up everything — specially personal security — take the road, experience the desert, live in contradiction and on the cross, in loneliness and fear, in pain and darkness and in the search for the invisible. But above all we must be conscious that Christ is alive and at our side on our journey. But Christ asks us to live in "genuine love".

A prophet of hope is a deeply realistic man; he understands and loves the historic moment and the men and women who surround him, neither hiding problems nor striving to shun sufferings. He is merely a contemplative man who teaches others that "sorrow will be turned into joy" and that "it was necessary to bear these sufferings to enter into glory".

139

But prophets are born: how is one to train them? "Before I formed you in the womb I knew you, and before you were born I consecrated you; I appointed you a prophet to the nations" (Jer 1:5). I would insist on these three points:

— teach him to *live in his time:* that is, to understand, love and share intensely in history with its demands and risks, its riches and challenges. It is to live intensely the life of the present day of the Incarnation;

— help him to enter deeply into the *paschal mystery* in its completeness: death and resurrection, sacrifice to the Father and giving life for friends, cross and hope, annihilation and exaltation, reconciliation of the world with the Father and deep fellowship with the brethren, liberation from every form of slavery (first that of sin) and creation of the *new man;*

— teach him to live in *"genuine love".* Only he who truly loves God — as one who has truly had experience of him — feels compelled to communicate his wonders to the world. And only he who truly loves humankind feel the urgency to understand men and women, to be with them and to cry to them: "Do not be afraid. It is I. Why did you doubt?".

A prophet of hope is not a comfortable man who confines himself merely to pointing the path. He is a "seer" who suffers misunderstanding and intrigue — true sign of opposition — and who pledges himself to take with his brothers and sisters the way of the cross and of life.

Conclusion

Training the priest of tomorrow — teacher of prayer, principle of fellowship and prophet of hope — is certainly not an easy task, nor humanly speaking to be desired. Trainers, now even they, need a word of hope: "Father, sanctify them in the truth; thy word is truth" (Jn 17:17). The first to be involved is Christ, who calls by love and sends to the mission. God works wonders in the poor. The trainer must live in poverty, contemplation and service. The others will be trained by the handing on of his own life, with the serene irradiation of the paschal joy of his own priesthood, and with the daily simplicity of a man who feels himself truly a "father" and loves his brethren with "genuine love".

May the Madonna of Advent — she who hopes serenely and gives gladly — may she help us to share joyfully in the priestly mystery of her Son, "a merciful high priest in the service of God" (Heb 2:17), "Mediator of a better covenant" (Heb 8:6), who has chosen us to announce his kingdom, celebrate his Easter and prophetically prepare his coming.

REFLECTIONS ON THE CONTEMPLATIVE LIFE

> Come away by yourselves to a
> lonely place and rest awhile
> (Mk 6:31).

Introduction

TO UNDERSTAND anything about the contemplative life one must at once take up a position in the vision of faith. Only on that level is it possible to discover the wealth and fruitfulness of this primary vocation in the church. "He went up into the hills, and called to him those whom he desired; and they came to him" (Mk 3:13). This text, of immediate application to apostles, has a strong inspiration for contemplation. Christ calls from the hill, after a long night of prayer (Lk 6:12-13), he calls in a free, unique way, so that the apostles may live in fellowship with him and thus be able to proclaim the kingdom and heal the sick.

If we wished to proclaim everything in human fashion and adapt it superficially to our schemes of quick returns, we should run the risk of losing the freshness of the mystery. "To you it is given to know the secrets of the kingdom". "Not all can understand these things". Therefore it is very important, in view of the mystery of the contemplative life, to take up an attitude of humility and respect, of admiration, poverty and gratitude.

Let us thank God for the gift of the contemplative life in the church of today: the church of the incarnation and the presence, of prophecy and service, of the evangelising mission and full liberation in Christ Jesus.

We cannot understand the contemplative life if we start from purely human experience; it is essentially a deep and meaningful experience of God. Nor can we understand it by the urgency of an immediate apostolic activity alone. Not everyone in the church must do everything and do it in the same way. That would be denying the multiform action of the Spirit and the differing richness of the body of Christ.

The contemplative life is a special way of practising the radical following of Christ in the desert. "He was led by the Spirit ... in the wilderness" (Lk 4: 1). It is a special way of making real and showing to the world the transforming fecundity of the Beatitudes.

I. Essential elements

In order to understand the essence and present state of the contemplative life, I think that we should emphasise these three elements: the desert, the word and the community:

a) *The desert:* as a place of revelation of and communication with God, as a very deep and unique experience of the love of God, and as a place of struggle and temptation, of trial and loyalty. One should discover what the desert meant in the lives of Moses, Elijah and Jesus.

One should also discover what this desert means today for the contemporary mind, specially for the younger generations. Is the desert a refuge, a parenthesis in life, a fleeting moment, a vacuum or an absence? Or is it a moment of greater spiritual fulfilment and a privileged place of meeting?

If the desert meant merely a simple "escape from the world" it would be the emptiest, most desolate and dreadful place. The human person is not born to be solitary. God has made us essentially to communicate and to give. Only thus is our human-divine vocation realised. It is one

143

thing to feel desolately lonely (the horrid meeting with the void, and personal struggle) and quite another to live, in solitude and silence, in the privileged, ineffable presence of him who tells us everything and does everything. For this reason, a contemplative who spends his solitude in a fruitful manner is a person who constantly experiences the joy of a double presence: God's gift and humankind's expectation. The contemplative knows that the Lord awaits him in the desert, and that the world is desperately in need of this meeting so that it may be enlightened, pacified and saved.

b) *The word:* in the desert the word is listened to, received and brought to life. To lisen to the word is not only to read and understand it, but basically to savour it at heart, in all the depth of its richness and the responsibility of its effectiveness. This word is not said merely for us to enjoy it, but so that we may know how to bear fruit from what we have contemplated. There are moments when it comes to us with a particularly prophetic urgency: it has to be communicated to others, to the church and to the world. Normally the word of God does not come to us to make us feel selfishly happy and safe: it comes to make us essentially witnesses and prophets. It is a word which must be welcomed in poverty, enjoyed in contemplative silence and put into practice without hesitation.

There is a specially privileged and responsible moment in regard to the word: when it must be brought into being in the church and proclaimed to the world. It is when the word (spoken or written) is pronounced by the pope, a bishop or a priest. It is always born of the virginal fecundity of a contemplative soul.

This word must be welcomed in poverty. "I thank thee, Father ... that thou hast hidden these things from the wise and understanding and revealed them to babes" (Lk 10:21). Only those who are "poor in spirit" enter into the depth of the word. Thus, true poverty is an indispensable condition for contemplation. However it is also true that contemplation must "normally" be nourished, whence follows the necessity of reading, study, personal and community reflection, and of the need to keep in constant touch with reality. There is a danger of contemplative communities impoverishing themselves and growing old, for lack of authentic intellectual renewal and of ecclesial and historical information brought up to date. That which determines the contemplative life is not separation from the world but exclusive attention to the word and total dedication to prayer. Separation from the world — shown by the enclosure — is only a means, not an end.

A contemplative monastery must make others share in the joy and saving fecundity of the word of God. Hence follows the need and urgency of adapting the hours and method of prayer so as to give others the chance of sharing in communal praying. Unfortunately, there are cases in which outsiders are offered only the assurance that they are prayed for and the emotive spectacle of a service which is beautiful, but distant and incomprehensible. There is today, specially among young people, an eagerness to "participate" in prayer. We should therefore do all we can to make this possible.

   c) *The community:* as a privileged means whereby communication with the Lord is experienced and his word is heard.

It must be a very simple community, where only the Lord is sought. A true contemplative community is essentially a praying community, and that is a community which worships the Lord (seeks his glory and lives in the joy of sacrifice in his name) and celebrates, in the name of all the world, "the praise of his glory". Therefore it is a community which lives essentially in accordance with its specific identity, occupied in listening to the word of God and being a symbol of a humanity which feels the need to adore, give thanks and supplicate.

145

J

But this community must be firmly included in the reality of the church and of the world. Superficial and distracting curiosity is one thing, grave and wise information another. A contemplative must feel the need of knowing what is happening in the church and in the world. This too nourishes his contemplation and brings him necessarily to meditate on God's word.

There is one evident and palpable sign of a true contemplative community: it is the deep, serene joy which is born of the common experience of the love of God, of the communal enjoyment of his word and of the desire to communicate it to the brethren. Today the young need and demand the direct witness of a true joy born of fraternal fellowship, contemplation and the cross. Therefore, it is not for contemplatives to live divorced from profound experience of God in the desert, but neither can they at all feel themselves distant from their fellow creatures and show themselves indifferent to their joy, their search and their hope.

II. Present state of the contemplative life

It is important to understand the present value of the contemplative life, that is, its place in the church today as a clear and comprehensible answer to the needs of the present-day world, particularly as an answer to the expectations of the young. This faces us with the question as to whether monasteries have been renewed in accordance with the real requirements of the Spirit, not in order to make life easier and more comfortable, but to make it more authentically contemplative, more ready to hear God's word and to pray.

The church today insists on evangelisation. Will it perhaps have to open the gates of monasteries so that nuns — until now given up to prayer and hidden work — may leap, even they, into the task of proclaiming the Good News to the poor, catechising them and pointing out to

happiness — that can be taken care of by no one but contemplatives. If contemplation is genuine, it will certainly have a greater capacity for discovering the drama of humankind in its true depth. The contemplative does not confine himself to diagnosing wretchedness and injustice; he goes to the root of the problems and discovers their cause. Maybe he will not be able to remedy the evil at once, yet his prophetic existence denounces it. From the absolute reality of God, the contemplative calls men and women to repentance and fraternal fellowship.

A great human sensibility is needed to be a genuine contemplative, not only to have the capacity to know completely the problems of others but also to possess great inner freedom to take them on with saving serenity. Because of this the contemplative life is deeply involved in human history. I would say that to be authentic it has to be fed by the pain and joy of others. In this sense the contemplative is the most realistic and contemporary person of all; he is also the most serene and active. Perhaps the new world will have to be made basically by contemplatives. They are the only ones, in the end, who stand at a distance from the immediate, go to the heart of the reality of problems, and possess a special capacity for seeing far ahead and building with patience. In this sense the contemplative life requires a great evangelical realism; the reality of God and his word above all, but also of the human person and his history. He is not a contemplative who simply ignores what is happening in the world; he is a contemplative who really listens to the Lord in the desert and in consequence knows how to understand and share in the pain of his brothers and sisters. Knowledge of the human person feeds contemplation; and contemplation deepens knowledge of the human person.

I think of some elements which the contemplative may well offer to the world of today, specially to the young, with a view to the integral development of peoples: the concept of the true liberty of the children of God, the fundamental experience of the divine fatherhood (the love of God), and, consequently, of universal brotherhood, the balance resulting from silence and prayer, the communication of peace and of joy, and the lasting communal witness of hope.

III. Fundamental requirements

I would like now to point out some fundamental requirements for a genuine contemplative life: love, silence, and poverty.

a) First of all *love*. "Let your love be genuine" (Rom 12:9). This involves seeking God above all things, entering into the "school of Jesus Christ", and allowing oneself to be strongly guided by the Holy Spirit. The same love involves being very much at the disposal of persons. The contemplative life is neither an escape nor a refuge; it is essentially a meeting with God and the brethren in the fullest possible way. Anyone who goes into the contemplative life out of fear of the world or to enjoy the word and the presence of the Lord for himself or herself alone, will never succeed in becoming a true contemplative. Contemplation is a privileged form of love; in a way it is the anticipation in time of the fullness of love in eternity. It could be said that action ceases (like faith and hope), but that contemplation remains. Not only that, but also that eternity will be pure active contemplation. "We shall see him as he is" (1 Jn 3:2). Or as St Augustine said: "There we shall rest and see, we shall see and love, we shall love and praise" (*City of God*, XXII, 30).

I am anxious to emphasise that the important thing is "to seek the kingdom of God and his righteousness" and that "Mary has chosen the better part". The contemplative life must be a clear witness of the primacy of

God's love and is worth the trouble of "losing one's life to take it up again". A very clear and simple sign of this love is the joy with which the contemplative life must normally express itself. The more one is living in contemplation in depth and in the serenity of the cross, the more normal and balanced it is. Balance is the fruit of contemplation: the true contemplative is the most normal and balanced of all persons — the most cheerful and realistic, the most expressive and communicative of hope.

Love becomes essentially clarity in prayer, fruitfulness of the cross and joy in fraternal fellowship. We must avoid the danger that material separation from the world — even the sign of that separation — should turn to contempt or ignorance of those who remain outside. Some ways of showing this particular vocation to live in the desert, with Christ and in men's hearts, would need to be revised.

b) *Silence* is absolutely essential for an authentic contemplative life. So, the contemplative life must be a very clear sign that the Word of God came into the world "in the fullness of silence". There must be a real atmosphere of silence within the monastery and around it. Those who enter a monastery know that the principal task of those who live there is to dedicate themselves to prayer and that this is their specific way of building the kingdom and of creating an evangelising, missionary church. It is the only way, and a most privileged way, for them to make history. Those who go to a monastery know also that they are not going merely to look for doctrine or advice, but to meet a Person.

Therefore, in a monastery it is essential to respect periods of silence and prayer. That is the basic meaning of the enclosure. The enclosure is not a place of protection but a means for a meeting — with God, with oneself and with others. The enclosure does not cause contemplation automatically; it helps it and draws attention to it. The enclosure is not a dividing and segregating line; it merely shows where the place of real encounter begins. It is a sign of the peace-making urgency of the desert.

However, this contemplative silence fundamentally requires two things; it must be a real meeting with the word who is Christ and with the transforming action of the Holy Spirit. Otherwise a fearful loneliness and a grievous void would be felt (it would at once produce the boredom of monotony and the impression of delusion); and, secondly, that the fruit of this silence should in some way be shared. The fruits of contemplation must be passed on; not always in a direct way (by word of mouth), but rather by shared praying. Today we notice a providential hunger for prayer among the young. Priests, men and women religious and the laity in general feel the need to go to contemplative monasteries to pray, not only to find a place of relaxation and tranquillity, and not only to ask the nuns for prayers, but to learn to pray and, still more, to pray together. In a monastery contemplative prayer must not offer principally an aesthetic spectacle, but an example, a way of communicating with the Father.

c) *Poverty* is an indispensable condition for prayer; it is one of the constituent elements of evangelical hope. The first characteristic of poverty in a contemplative monastery is that of not feeling oneself a master of contemplation in the church (as also religious cannot feel themselves the masters of prophecy). In the world there are people who are deeply contemplative. The enclosure is not identified with contemplation, nor does it produce it automatically.

Contemplation is essentially a work of the Holy Spirit; we must ask for it with humility and wait for it with a pure heart. Neither must we, meanwhile, feel that we are the exclusive owners of the basic charism, nor tie ourselves materially down to fixed forms for showing or securing separation from the world. I would like to repeat once more that the essential in the contemplative life is not separation from the world, but a real meeting with Jesus Christ. To reach this, poverty is necessary: in the sense of a total casting off of human security (goods, people, traditions) and a sincere search for the Lord in prayer. The Lord reveals himself to the simple and to the humble. There are in fact deeply contemplative souls among the poor, or, better, the true poor are deeply contemplative. Speaking of the poor in connection with the contemplative life makes us think of certain concrete situations which frequently occur today in not a few communities. One is the witness that contemplative monasteries can today give to contemporary thinking, specially among the young. We know that within the monasteries lives are lived in hard and joyful austerity and at times in subhuman conditions. Yet the arrangement of the monastery is not a witness easily understood by the world of today. Should we not think of new ways of building our monasteries, less apparently sumptuous and, for a change, more functional and suitable for the contemplative life? For there are things which are today superfluous for monasteries and others which they miss. The normal mental make-up of a contemplative requires a certain period of personal solitude and a greater possibility of getting in touch with God in nature.

Another aspect of poverty is the desire to betake oneself into poor, "fringe" districts, to live a genuine contemplative life there, making common cause with the poor and teaching them really to hope. It is not a matter of suppressing the essential of the contemplative life (experience of God in the desert, life of silence and prayer, some basic signs of special isolation from the world, exclusive dedication to the enjoyment of the word of God without immediate reference to fixed apostolic activity). But it is a matter of giving the poor an opportunity of contemplative prayer. A simple monastery, organised soberly and poorly in a marginal or rural neighbourhood and easily accessible to all, can be a witness to God and an effective means of evangelisation.

Conclusion

I should like to end these simple reflections — which are nothing more than a plain ordinary meditation — with a short reference to two positive phenomena which are appearing in the church today, concerning the contemplative life.

The first is that, whereas in some parts it would seem that there are fewer contemplative vocations and communities are getting old, it is fortunate that in other parts many clear signs exist of young, mature and zealous vocations. It could be said that the characteristic of these vocations is seriousness, balance, joy, a deep sense of the church, hunger for prayer and the absolute reality of God coupled with a real sense of the human person and an evangelical awareness of the problems of history.

The second is the rise of many new and lively forms of the contemplative life, which, on the one hand, seek with greater intensity the absolute reality of God and the desert and, on the other, keep themselves very wide awake to the needs and expectations of society. These are evident manifestations of the transforming action of the Holy Spirit who is calling the church today to a life of deep contemplation and authentic prophecy. We are living, therefore, in a privileged and hopeful era. May it be God's will for us to know how to profit from it! May we be always accompanied by Mary our Mother, the contemplative, who "kept all these things and pondered them" in the depth of her heart.

MEDITATION FOR TIMES
OF DIFFICULTY

> When these things begin to take place, look up and raise your heads, because your redemption is drawing near (Lk 21:28).

> I have said this to you, that in me you may have peace. In the world you have tribulation; but be of good cheer, I have overcome the world (Jn 16:33).

Introduction

WHEN certain things happen, in the church and in the world, it is logical for us to be worried and to suffer. At the least we have not met them vividly in our lives and we find it absurd that they happen after twenty centuries of Christianity. It would seem too that the very life of Christians is losing its evangelical effectiveness and may be ceasing to be the "salt of the earth and light of the world" (Mt 5:13-16). There is fratricidal strife, and an increase in kidnapping and murder, hatreds, persecutions and violence. All this produces fear and mistrust, anxiety, and pessimism. Why do these things happen? Will there not be someone who can put to flight the temptation of violence and the paralysing sensation of fear?

Within the church itself — till now the prototype of all which is sacred and intangible, which is uniquely and really solid and stable — we have seen the emergence of strife and criticism, disunity among Christians, danger of secularism and the turning of the gospel into politics, loss of direction by many, loss of one's own identity in the consecrated life, and the danger of breaking unity of doctrine and discipline — and all this in the name of Jesus Christ and for loyalty to his gospel!

Others, on the other hand, with lamentable superficiality, accuse the church of having departed a long way from its evangelising mission, without, unfortunately, understanding that the church, in line with Christ who was sent by the Father, has been consecrated by the Spirit to announce the Good News to the poor, liberty to the prisoners and sight to the blind (Lk 4:18). The church must explicitly proclaim Jesus Christ, the Saviour, and the coming of his kingdom, must call men and women to repentance and faith and must transform the human person and the whole of humanity (EN 18). But evangelisation "would not be complete if it did not take account of the intimate connection between the gospel and the concrete, personal and social life of the individual" (EN 29).

Without doubt we are living in difficult times; it is useless to complain, and yet more useless, even more disastrous, to want to ignore it as if all were going well, or to allow oneself definitely to shrug it off as if it were impossible to do anything about it. But within all this — we know it infallibly by faith — it is God who controls history, it is Christ who presides over the church, and it is the Holy Spirit who brings new times to birth in pain by the final creation. Further, if believing costs dearly, it is absolutely certain — as much for individuals as for the life of our communities — that "if any one is in Christ, he is a new creation; the old has passed away, behold, the new has come. All this is from God, who through Christ reconciled us to himself and gave us the ministry of reconciliation" (2 Cor 5:17-18). For these reasons, I feel the need to meditate once more, but very simply, on hope, without wishing to conduct a too technical analysis of the word of God, or professing to study in depth, historically and sociologically, the root of the evil. That can be done by others of greater competence, and it is necessary for them to do it. I want merely to offer some reflections on the present distress, in the light of the word of God. I desire, that is to say, to start a simple meditation which may help us, on the one hand, to make a realistic appraisal of the present sad and distressing reality, and, on the other, to find in it the providence of the Father, the passage of the Lord in history and the continuously re-creative activity of the Holy Spirit. It will not, then, be an exhaustive study of the present situation, nor a complete analysis of the texts of holy scripture. It is just a meditation aloud on christian hope in difficult times, which may help us all to free ourselves from paralysing fear and to allow ourselves to be filled by the Spirit of power who makes us witnesses and martyrs.

It is ultimately a matter of seeing how difficult times belong to the Father's plan and are essentially times of grace and salvation; to see further how Jesus lived in difficult times which are essential to his redemptive mission, and how he overcame them by virtue of the paschal mystery. Jesus' Magna Carta for overcoming difficult times is the Sermon on the Mount. The culminating moment is his death on the cross and his resurrection. His principal preaching is the call to universal love, to the spirit of the Beatitudes and to the fruitfulness of the cross. So Jesus opens to us the way to living through difficult times with love and gratitude and to turning them into providential times of hope.

Treating it as a meditation, I should like to end this introduction with three clear and simple texts: from the Prophet, from the Apostle and from Christ. Isaiah, the prophet of hope, tells us in the name of the Lord: "Strengthen the weak hands, and make firm the feeble knees. Say to those who are of a fearful heart, 'Be strong, fear not! Behold, your God will come with vengeance, with the recompense of God. He will come and save you'" (Is 35:3-4). In the Acts of the Apostles we read this sentence said by the Lord to St Paul, the apostle of hope: "Do not be afraid, but speak and do not be silent; for I am with you, and no man shall attack you to harm you" (Acts 18:9-10). Finally Christ, "our blessed hope" (Tit

2:13) recommends calm and boldness before inevitable and providential difficult times to us: "Why are you afraid? Have you no faith?" (Mk 4:40), "Take heart, it is I. Have no fear" (Mk 6:50).

How necessary it is in difficult times, to have the certainty that Christ is the Lord of history, who remains with his church to the end and who goes with us as we complete the road to the Father! How important it is to remember that it is precisely for difficult times that God has pledged his presence! "Go into all the world and preach the gospel to the whole creation"; "Lo, I am with you always, to the close of the age" (Mk 16:15; Mt 28:20). "You will be hated by all for my name's sake. But not a hair of your head will perish" (Lk 21:12-18).

I. "Always be ready to render account for the hope that is in you" (1 Pet 3:15)

"The people who walked in darkness have seen a great light; those who dwelt in a land of deep darkness, on them has light shined" (Is 9:2). On Christmas night the liturgy invites us to joy and to hope. Isaiah thus describes, in the gloomy darkness of difficult times, the coming of Christ who is Light, Peace and Covenant. "For to us a child is born, to us a son is given ... his name will be called Prince of Peace" (Is 9:6). Jesus Christ came to proclaim peace to us: "He is our peace ... he came and preached peace to you who were far off and peace to those who were near" (Eph 2:14-18). He came, above all, to bring us peace as the fruit of his Easter: "Peace I leave with you; my peace I give to you; not as the world gives do I give to you. Let not your hearts be troubled, neither let them be afraid" (Jn 14:27). The peace which Christ brings us is always the fruit of a cross. Christ has "reconciled to himself all things ... making peace by the blood of his cross" (Col 1:20). The whole gospel is an invitation to inner calm, to planned concord of nations, and to the joy of fraternal love. "This I command you, to love one another" (Jn 15:17). But the Lord always spoke of difficult times; for himself and for us. He never predicted easy or comfortable times to his disciples. On the contrary, he required of them a very clear choice of poverty, fraternal love and the cross. "If any man would come after me, let him deny himself and take up his cross daily and follow me" (Lk 9:23). To the scribe who felt superficially inclined to follow him, Jesus replied: "Foxes have holes, and birds of the air have nests; but the Son of man has nowhere to lay his head" (Mt 8:19-20). Jesus is a "sign that is spoken against" (Lk 2:34). The Christian follows his path: "A servant is not greater than his master; nor is he who is sent greater than he who sent him" (Jn 13:16). So we must necessarily live through the Passion of the Lord and accept with calmness and joy the demands of our following: "If the world hates you, know that it has hated me before it hated you … . Remember the word that I said to you: 'A servant is not greater than his master'. If they persecuted me, they will persecute you" (Jn 15:18-20).

All this, however, is lighted up by a note of realistic hope: "Truly, truly, I say to you, you will weep and lament, but the world will rejoice; you will be sorrowful, but your sorrow will turn into joy" (Jn 16:20). It has always been useful and necessary for there to be poor, strong individuals, with a great capacity for feeling the approach of dawn during the night, since they are living open to the Light, and who would know how to pass on to their own brothers and sisters the certainty of the presence of the Lord and of his imminent coming. "I am with you always, till the close of the age" (Mt 28:20), "Surely, I am coming soon" (Rev 22:20). Today more than ever we need prophets of hope, true prophets of real hope, those completely possessed by the Holy Spirit, in other words, disinterested contemplative persons who know how to live in the poverty, steadfastness and love of the Holy Spirit and who therefore are transformed into serene and ardent witnesses of Easter, who speak to us openly of the

Father, show us Jesus and communicate to us the gift of his Spirit. They are persons who can savour the cross like St Paul (Gal 6:14; Col 1:24) and so venture to preach to their own brethren that the unique strength and wisdom of God is in Christ crucified (1 Cor 1:23-24). The wisdom and power of the world count for nothing; only the fruition of the cross is of importance. All the rest is silliness and failure in God's plan. Christ was made "our wisdom, our righteousness and sanctification and redemption" (1 Cor 1:30). When it seems that everything is breaking up, within the church or in the heart of history, then joy and hope arise in the world. Christian hope is born of the inevitable and providential absurdity of the cross. It was necessary "that Christ should suffer these things and enter into his glory" (Lk 24:26). But christian hope is active and requires patience and boldness. Only the poor — the despoiled and naked, destitute according to the world but totally safe in God who does not come by measure — can truly hope.

Our times, in the church and in the world, are very difficult. Therefore they are also like those of the gospel. That means that "the kingdom of God is at hand" (Lk 21:32), and it is the time when the true Christian is called upon to "give an account of his hope" (1 Pet 3:15); that is to say, to penetrate by means of faith and the Holy Spirit into the scandal of the cross and to draw from it the irremovable certainty of Easter, so as to pass it on to others.

In difficult times there is a great deal of fear, sadness and discouragement and so violence increases. Violence is a sign of loss of the sight of truth, of forgetfulness of justice and of loss of love. Periods in which violence increases are the most miserable and barren times. By it a lack of spiritual strength is clearly shown; and then there is an attempt to replace it with the absurd use of force. Today we are living in times of conflict and violence, times, above all, in which every one thinks he has the right to make his own justice, because he believes that he alone possesses absolute truth, is entirely faithful to the gospel and unique in his struggle for human rights. This, in difficult times, is one of the gravest dangers, believing that one has understood Christ definitively. That is a denial of hope, according to the psychology and spirituality of St Paul: "Not that I have already obtained (the prize) or am already perfect; but I press on to make it my own, because Christ Jesus has made me his own. Brethren, I do not consider that I have made it my own, but ... I press onward toward the goal" (Phil 3:12-14).

Another serious obstacle, in difficult times, is the defeatist conscience, which maintains that it is impossible to overcome such difficulties. It is found among politicians and religious, mature men and women and adolescents, young people in the work force and university students. St Thomas defines the object of hope as a future good which is difficult but possible to reach (S.Th. 1, 2, 40, 1; 2, 2, 17, 1). So today more than ever a simple meditation on hope is necessary, not with the intention of consoling the superficial and sending their consciences to sleep, but with the desire to encourage the courageous, specially those who are young. It is for them, above all, to liberate tradition and build up the new world in hope: "I write to you, young men, because you are strong, and the word of God abides in you, and you have overcome the evil one" (1 Jn 2:14).

I think, as I write, of all Christians, those who by the mercy of the Father, through the resurrection of Jesus Christ from the dead, have been reborn to a lively hope (1 Pet 1:3). I think particularly of those who have been providentially countersigned with the cross and are called to bear witness to Jesus in extreme poverty, in persecution, in prison and in death. I think in a special way of bishops and priests, who are by definition, the primary witnesses of Easter (Acts 1:8), and, consequently, the essential prophets of hope. I think particularly, too, of men and women religious (and all consecrated souls) who, by their specific vocation, proclaim the final kingdom. They are, by divine choice, serene and light-giving prophets of hope.

I do not think exclusively of one particular country or continent. I take a wider view of the world and the suffering church. The pope and the bishops suffer; so do priests and laity, young religious and their elders, hungry and oppressed peoples, statesmen and the ordinary men and women in the street.

Times are difficult and humanly speaking absurd. So we must discover, appreciatae and live intensely in the providential and unrepeatable fruition of this hour. It is not the hour of the weak or cowardly, of those who have chosen Christ for the certainty of salvation or the recompense of reward, but the hour of the strong and bold in the Spirit, of those who have chosen the Lord for the honour of his name, the joy of his glory and the service of the brethren. It is the hour of witnesses and martyrs. Do not let us be frightened by sufferings! We have the light of hope for the new times: "I consider that the sufferings of this present time are not worth comparing with the glory that is to be revealed in us" (Rom 8:18).

It is not a matter, however, of living resigned to idle waiting for the new times, but instead of continuing to prepare for them in charity and justice. They are to be times of peace, whose characteristic is the "joy inspired by the Holy Spirit" (1 Thess 1:6). The God of all consolation "comforts us in all our affliction, so that we may be able to comfort those who are in any affliction, with the comfort with which we ourselves are comforted by God. For as we share abundantly in Christ's sufferings, so through Christ we share abundantly in comfort too ... . Our hope for you is unshaken" (2 Cor 1:3-7). For difficult times we need hope, that firm, creative hope of Christians which depends on "the love of God in Christ Jesus our Lord" (Rom 8:39), and which requires in us poverty, contemplation and the power of the Holy Spirit.

St Peter exhorts the Christians of his day: "Now who is there to harm you if you are zealous for what is right?

But even if you do suffer for righteousness' sake, you will be blessed. Have no fear of them, nor be troubled, but in your hearts reverence Christ as Lord. Always be prepared to make a defence to any one who calls you to account for the hope that is in you" (1 Pet 3:13-15).

II.   Christ Jesus our hope (1 Tim 1:1)

A simple meditation on hope must always start from a simple contemplation of Jesus Christ, "our blessed hope" (Tit 2:13), above all in his paschal mystery: it is there that Jesus finally overcame difficult times. As a result, the church lives today in dependence on the cross and sings of the certainty of her hope: "Hail, O Cross, our only hope" (Hymn at Vespers of the Passion); for the cross leads us definitively to the resurrection "Christ, my hope, is risen" (sequence of Easter). It is of interest, above all, to see how Christ overcame difficult times. The important thing about him is that he did not come to make an end of them, but to teach us to overcome them calmly, firmly and joyfully, just as he did not come to make an end of the cross but rather to give it meaning.

Christ was born in the fullness of difficult times. There is Mary. He came to bring us freedom and make us sons of the Father in the Spirit. The fullness of times, in the Father's plan, is marked by the fullness of the difficult: an acute consciousness of sin, of oppression and wretchedness, and the desire and hope of salvation. This is the time in which Jesus was born.

What Jesus reveals to us in the first place as a way of overcoming difficult times, is the Father's love and the meaning of his coming: "God so loved the world that he gave his only Son, that whoever believes in him should not perish but have eternal life. For God sent the Son into the world, not to condemn the world, but that the world might be saved through him" (Jn 3:16-17). Therefore, when Jesus was born, the angel announced joy and hope: "Be not afraid; for behold I bring you good news of a great joy which will come to all the people; for to you is born this day in the city of David a Saviour, who is Christ the Lord" (Lk 2:10-11). Christ came to speak to us plainly of the Father (Jn 16:25), to introduce us into the mystery of the kingdom (Mt 13:11) and to show us the way to true happiness (Mt 5:1-12). The Beatitudes are now the only way of changing the world and the clearest manifestation that difficult times can be turned into times of grace: "Behold, now is the acceptable time; behold, now is the day of salvation" (2 Cor 6:2). When Jesus wishes to teach us to live in hope and overcome difficult times he always suggests to us three fundamental attitudes: prayer, bearing the cross and fraternal love. They are three ways of entering into joyful fellowship with the Father. Therefore they are three ways to our feeling strong in him and experiencing the joy of serving our brethren. Yet, in the end, the first and essential attitude for living through and overcoming difficult times is trust in the Father's love: "The Father himself loves you" (Jn 16:27). The way for difficult times, in Jesus, is not fear, indifference or violence; on the contrary, it is the joy of love: "Love your enemies and pray for those who persecute you" (Mt 5:44), it is the balance and power of prayer: "Pray that you may not enter into temptation" (Mt 26:41), and it is the fruitful serenity of the cross: "Unless a grain of wheat falls into the earth and dies, it remains alone; but if it dies, it bears much fruit" (Jn 12:24).

History was marking the fullness of difficult times when Jesus was born. His redemptive incarnation was the realisation of the ancient hope and the beginning of the new and definitive hope. From the time when Jesus was born, and above all when, glorified at the right hand of the Father, he sent his Spirit into the world, we live in the time of hope. It will be finally consummated when Jesus returns to assign the kingdom to the Father (1 Cor 15:25-28).

St Paul summarises it wonderfully, in a text which,

very significantly, we read on Christmas night: "The grace of God has appeared for the salvation of all men, training us to renounce irreligion and worldly passions, and to live sober, upright and godly lives in this world, awaiting our blessed hope, the appearing of the great God and Saviour Jesus Christ, who gave himself for us" (Tit 2:11-14). In other words, hope shines in the world when Jesus is born and dies for humankind. The way and certainty of hope are very different in God's plan and in human calculations. Hope, in the mystery of Christ, starts with humiliation, annihilation and death: wherefore the Father was to glorify him and give him a name above every other name (Phil 2:7-9). Christ experienced fear, grief and anguish before the approach of difficult times: "He began to be sorrowful and troubled" (Mt 26:37); "He began to be greatly distressed and troubled" (Mk 14:33). It was a fear, grief and anguish of death. He sought to overcome the difficult moment in the serene intensity of prayer as joyful communion with the will of his Father: "Being in an agony he prayed more earnestly; and his sweat became like great drops of blood falling down upon the ground" (Lk 22:39-44). Yet, the Lord feels the importance, the fruitfulness and the joy of difficult times: "Now is my soul troubled. And what shall I say? Father save me from this hour? No, for this purpose I have come to this hour" (Jn 12:27).

Yet this does not mean that the Lord was seeking to put himself into difficult circumstances or to anticipate his hour for his own sake. "So they took up stones to throw at him; but Jesus hid himself, and went out of the temple" (Jn 8:59). That he did, not in order to escape difficult times and because he did not wish to bend his shoulders to the cross; he did it solely "because his hour had not yet come" (Jn 7:30). He counsels the same generosity and wisdom before the cross to his disciples. He does not tell them to expect easy paths; indeed he announces difficult times, but recommends evangelical prudence: "Behold, I send you out as sheep in the midst

165

of wolves; so be wise as serpents and innocent as doves" (Mt 10:16).

There are particularly difficult moments in the life of Jesus, such, for example, as the rejection by his own people: "He came to his own home, and his own people received him not" (Jn 1:11). Such too was the division among his disciples and the desertion of some of them because his "saying was hard". That must have been one of the saddest moments in the Lord's life: "After this many of his disciples drew back and no longer went about with him" (Jn 6:66). But undoubtedly the really difficult hour for Jesus is the hour of his Passion. It was eagerly desired by him, three times foretold to his disciples, greatly feared, but intensely loved and welcomed: "The hour has come for the Son of man to be glorified. Truly, truly, I say to you, unless a grain of wheat falls into the earth and dies, it remains alone; but if it dies, it bears much fruit" (Jn 12:24). Thus Jesus teaches us to overcome difficult times. Through his unconditional dedication to the Father on the cross he converts death into life, sorrow into joy, slavery into freedom, darkness into light, division into unity, sin into grace, violence into peace, and despair into hope. Jesus does not annihilate difficult times, no more does he make them easy; he simply converts them into grace. He makes us see the Father showing himself in them and invites us to accept them in the hope that is born from the cross.

To understand how Jesus lived and overcame difficult times through the mystery of the paschal cross, we must meditate simply and lovingly on St Paul's famous hymn on Christ's glorification through his annihilation in the Incarnation, his obedience to the death on the cross and his exaltation as Lord of all things (Phil 2:6-11).

This is the Christ who is today living in the church. For this reason the church, the sacrament of the Easter Christ, is the true sign of hope in the every-day world. He made it so when, from the bosom of the Father, he sent the promised Holy Spirit, who dwells in, gives life to, and unifies, the church. Pentecost, the completion of Easter, is the manifestation of the mastery of Jesus, and the assurance that the church, indwelt by the Spirit, will overcome difficult times. The church prolongs Christ's passion in time until it reaches completion (Col 1:24). The Lord had foretold it: "The hour is coming when whoever kills you will think he is offering service to God" (Jn 16:2). The sad thing in the church is when brethren confront each other with violence, when they persecute each other, imprison and kill each other in the name of God. It is not the moment for despair; it is a case of remembering the Lord's words: "In the world you have tribulation; but be of good cheer, I have overcome the world" (Jn 16:33). Difficult times are always conquered by the fullness of love, the fruitfulness of the cross and the transforming power of the gospel Beatitudes.

III. The transforming power of hope: being poor

"Blessed are the poor in spirit, for theirs is the kingdom of heaven" (Mt 5:3).

To face difficult times and overcome them with the fertility of love and the transforming power of hope it is necessary to be poor. We had put our trust too much in technology, science and human strength. We have discovered the individual and his history, time and the world but we have forgotten God and lost the vision of the eternal. We have felt too sure of ourselves. Therefore, the first condition for truly hoping is to be poor. Only the poor, who do not feel sure of themselves, without right to anything and with ambition for nothing know how to hope. They put all their trust in God alone and are content with what they have. The true poor are never violent but they are the only ones who possess the secret of deep changes. That may perhaps seem an illusion but it is not so if we put ourselves in the perspective of the Father's

167

plan, incomprehensible to us, and of the action of the Spirit. Let us not forget that the fruits of the Spirit are love, joy and peace (Gal 5:22).

Difficult times occur when things or persons shut us in, when they limit our freedom, obscure the horizon and prevent our being faithful to God's plan and the realisation of our divine vocation. Difficult times began when the devil made creatures lose their freedom with the excuse that they would become like God (Gen 3:5). Therefore, the time of hope begins when the Son of God empties himself of the manifestation of his glory and makes himself a servant, obedient unto death and the death on the cross (Phil 2:8). The despoiling of Christ, his annihilation and death, open to us the path to wealth and freedom. "Though he was rich, yet for your sake he became poor, so that by his poverty you might become rich" (2 Cor 8:9). So Christ frees us from sin and from death (Rom 8:2). He came to make us free (Gal 5:1), taking away by his death "the sin of the world" (Jn 1:29).

A clear demonstration of the lack of poverty is being sure of oneself and despising others: "God, I thank thee that I am not like other men" (Lk 8:11). It is the same sin of excessive self-confidence that, even in the midst of his sincere love for the Master, makes St Peter run into danger and makes him fall: "Though they all fall away because of you, I will never fall away" (Mt 26:33). Ultimately, the rich man who feels sure of himself, has no need of the Lord. Because of this, he will never be able truly to believe in God whose essence is kindness and the mercy of forgiveness. St Paul's solemn confession of faith is interesting in this respect: "The saying is sure and worthy of full acceptance that Christ Jesus came into the world to save sinners. And I am the foremost of sinners" (1 Tim 1:15). When one feels oneself poor and wretched, God makes himself specially near and intimate. The clear and serene consciousness of one's own limits and wretchedness enables Jesus Christ, the Saviour to enter into one. In Mary in her poverty the Omnipotent works marvels and Holy is his name (Lk 1:48-49). And through this, Mary, the lowly handmaid of the Lord, changed history.

It is interesting to notice that times turn out to be specially difficult when a person thinks that he has the infallible key for the solution of all problems; when, for example, some in the church believe that they are the only poor people who have understood the gospel, who have discovered the secret of being nearer and more open to Jesus Christ and who are really involved in the liberation of humankind, while others feel that they are the only people faithful to the wealth of tradition and consider themselves infallible teachers of their fellows. Or even in secular society, when some think that the rest have done nothing and that they themselves have the only formula for transforming the world. The frequent failure of human beings, with the consequent disillusion of the young, ought to be a call to poverty, which is not only a christian virtue, but a virtue which is necessary and of really primary importance for great men and women. Tensions often have their source and origin in a claim to have exclusive rights in truth and holiness. Peace is the possession of willing hearts only; and willingness implies poverty. Christian hope depends on the omnipotence and kindness of God. To depend upon God one must be poor. Christian poverty is a complete dispossession of oneself, of things and of persons. It is hunger for God, necessity of prayer and humble trust in the brethren. Therefore Mary, who was poor, trusted so much in the Lord and pledged her loyalty to his word (Lk 1:38). Mary's song is the cry of hope of the poor.

This same meditation on hope for difficult times must necessarily be kept on a line of poverty and is therefore extremely simple. If it claimed to be technical or to exhaust the subject, or to teach it to others or to want to correct them, it would cease to be a manifestation of God to the poor. It would cease to be poor. Its intention is to be no more than a simple communication of God to re-awaken the profound truth which has been sown in the

169

L

hearts of men and women, and a preparation for receiving the complete truth which is Christ (Jn 16:33).

Hope is a strong virtue, but at the same time it is joyful and serene. In this it is similar to poverty, which, if real, is strong but not aggressive; in some circumstances it is very sad, but it never ceases to be serene and joyful. The poor man hopes in the Lord more than the watchman for the dawn (Ps 130:5-6), and keeps his eyes fixed on the Lord as the eyes of a maid look to the hands of her mistress (Ps 123:2).

Poverty and hope make our desires and security centre in Jesus Christ. Poverty lays us open to Jesus Christ our Saviour. Hope makes us strain to meet him. It also makes us think of Mary, who sums up the "small remnant" of the "poor" who waited for salvation in Israel. In Mary, in her poverty, was completed the fullness of time, and so she is the Mother of holy hope.

IV. Hope and contemplation

"Rejoice in your hope, be patient in tribulation, be constant in prayer" (Rom 12:12).

Only the contemplative really knows how to hope. For the illusion of what is immediate may make us lose the reality of the profound and the presence of the definitive. Hope is precisely this: the anticipated fruition of the future; just as eternity will be the ultimate fruition of what is hoped for. Even in this we find the Beatitudes are relevant: only the pure in heart have the ability to see God (Mt 5:8).

Hope presupposes a great deal of inner poise. As a rule we get anxious and feel despair when we have no time or quiet for praying. Monks and nuns not only calm us because they are a sign of what must come (the future good that we are waiting for), but above all because they introduce us into the invisible things of God and make us experience his presence. The experience of God inundates us with the joy of hope (Rom 12:12). It is a fearful thing, in fact, when a monk leaves contemplation for the attraction of the illusion that he can change the world by a flurry of activity. His proper way of changing the world, building history and saving humankind is to continue to be deeply contemplative, a true man of God and teacher of prayer, that is a genuine seer.

There is no doubt that contemplation does not mean forgetting history nor escaping world problems. It would be an absurd way of pleasing oneself, leaving the Lord always in twilight. True contemplation is a gift of the Holy Spirit. It is followed only with purity of heart and the hunger of the poor. Contemplation makes us discover God's plan and the Lord's passage in history and the incessant, creative activity of the Spirit. A true contemplative makes us understand three things: that it is only God who matters, that Jesus lives among us and accompanies us on our pilgrimage towards the Father, and that eternity has begun and we are advancing with Christ to the consummation of the kingdom (1 Cor 15:24). Contemplation continually reveals to us Christ who is "our hope" (1 Tim 1:1). It brings the Lord to us in difficult moments: "It is I, have no fear" (Mk 6:50). It makes us available to the brethren: "As you did it to ... my brethren, you did it to me" (Mt 25:40).

There are aspects of special interest to hope which are easily understandable by contemplatives; entering into invisible good things, tasting in advance the good things of eternity, the nearness and indwelling of the omnipotent good God, the evaluation of time and human beings, the presence of Jesus Christ in history, the motive power of creation until its final recapitulation in Christ (Rom 8:18-25; Eph 1:10), and the continually creative activity of the Holy Spirit who dwells in us and will revive our mortal bodies (Rom 8:11), making them like the glorious body of our Lord Jesus Christ (Phil 3:21). Hope is essentially a journey towards the ultimate meeting with the

Lord (1 Thess 4:17) making us depend upon the God who has been revealed to us in Jesus Christ.

But, in order to hope truly, we must live in fellowship; charity is therefore essential to christian hope (St Thomas 2, 2, 17, 3). There are even occasions when we need to hope with the hope of friends. When weariness and discouragement make us weaken, like Elijah in the wilderness, there is always someone who cries to us in the name of the Lord: "Arise and walk, for you have a long way to go" (cf. 1 Kg 19:7). Contemplation is this capacity for immediately finding the presence of the Lord in friends who are God's instruments, like the despairing disciples of Emmaus who recognised him in the breaking of the bread (Lk 24:35).

Difficult times must, therefore, be entered into by depth of contemplation. We must look at them from a distance and basically. Thus we shall find out the cause of the evil: why such things happen. Contemplation above all lets us find out every feature of God's saving plan in the midst of absurd and disconcerting human events. By means of contemplation we are assured that what is impossible for human beings, becomes possible only in God. It is important to understand that God's way are mysterious and do not coincide with those of this world as a rule. If things turn out difficult it is because creatures contort and change the Lord's ways. We are always impressed by Paul's attitude in the Acts of the Apostles: "The Spirit of Jesus did not allow them" (Acts 16:7).

However, above all, contemplation makes us listen humbly and obediently to the word of God: there is communicated to us, always in chiaroscuro of the faith, what God requires of us, why certain things happen, and what we ought to do to change history. Mary changed the story of slavery to the story of freedom: of that freedom wherewith Christ has made us free (Gal 5:1) by her humble willingness as handmaid of the Lord.

Contemplation puts us in lively contact with the word of God; it is there that we savour the story of salvation and learn to appreciate how God has "visited and redeemed his people" (Lk 1:68). In contemplation of the word of God we understand in actual fact how God was able to separate the waters for the chosen people to pass through (Ex 14:21-23), and then join them up again so as to bury their pursuers; and how a young shepherd without armour could bring down with a sling-shot the giant who was threatening the people (1 Sam 17:49). We understand, above all, how there are no moments impossible for God, that we must wait patiently, and that salvation comes to us from what is humanly hopeless: "Can anything good come out of Nazareth?" (Jn 1:46; cf. 1 Cor 1:27-28).

Contemplatives have a great capacity for continually recreating the word of God in the Spirit, bringing it surprisingly up to date, so that we do not pessimistically think that there is nothing more to do and that our times are the most obscure and difficult in history.

St John, the contemplative, wrote in difficult times to the young men of his day: "I write to you, young men, because you are strong, and the word of God abides in you, and you have overcome the evil one" (1 Jn 2:14). Will it not be for this reason perhaps that today the young love contemplation more than ever and are going in search of the desert and the fruition of the word? Will it not perhaps be because they know in actual life the difficulties of the times and that the only way of overcoming them is to arm themselves with strength in the Spirit and allow God's word to dwell in their hearts by contemplation? Difficult times are suitable for the poverty, the contemplation and the courage of the young; so they are the most suitable for their hope.

Contemplation helps us to decipher the mystery of the cross and overcome its scandal and foolishness (1 Cor 1:23); it makes us conquer fear and despair because it helps us to enjoy the gladness and fecundity of sufferings (Gal 6:14; Col 1:24; Jn 12:24). Fear, anxiety and sorrow can co-exist temporarily with contemplation. They did co-exist in the painfully serene depth of Christ's prayer in the garden (Lk 22:39ff.). However, everything was immediately solved in unconditional, absolute and entirely filial abandonment to the Father's will; "not as I will, but as thou wilt" (Mt 26:39). We learn thus that prayer is very simple and calm, that it is merely entering into communion with the adorable will of the Father: "Yes, Father, for such was thy gracious will" (Lk 10:21).

Contemplation gives us inner poise because it puts us into immediate touch with Jesus Christ who is "our peace" (Eph 2:14) and with his Spirit, who cries in our silence "with sighs too deep for words" (Rom 8:26) and makes us enjoy the Father's secrets. It plunges us into the depth of love, and love chases out fear (1 Jn 4:18). We find one of the most profoundly human experiences in fear. Yet Jesus Christ came to free us from fear; therefore he himself was temporarily subjected to the experience of fear (Mk 14:33), but he asked us not be afraid (Jn 14:1, 27). The experience of fear is fundamentally good, christian and suitable for poor people. What is not christian is the distress of a fear which destroys and para- lyses, which shuts the heart away from fellowship with the brethren and from simple filial trust in God the Father. For this reason the gospel of salvation and grace is a con- tinual invitation to calm, a permanent exhortation not to be afraid: the Annunciation (Lk 1:30), the Nativity (Lk 2:10), the Resurrection (Mt 28:10). "Do not fear". "Do not be afraid".

V. **Firmness and hope**

"We rejoice in our sufferings, knowing that suffering produces endurance, and endurance produces character, and character produces hope, and hope does not disappoint us, because God's love has been poured into our hearts through the Holy Spirit who has been given to us" (Rom 5:3-5).

St Paul feels, like Jesus Christ, the glory and the fertility of suffering. "Far be it from me to glory except in the cross" (Gal 6:14). It is the cross inwardly and outwardly, accepted with joy for the church and for the world: "Now I rejoice in my sufferings for your sake, and in my flesh I complete what is lacking in Christ's afflictions for the sake of his body, that is, the church" (Col 1:24). This same act of suffering for Christ he desires at heart for his sons and daughters whom he implores to continue to be "worthy of the gospel of Christ ... not frightened in anything by your opponents ... for it is granted to you that for the sake of Christ you should not only believe in him but also suffer for his sake" (Phil 1:27-30).

However this deep gladness in suffering is linked with firmness of hope. And hope, in turn, takes its own strength from the love of the Father manifested in Christ Jesus (Rom 8:39) and communicated to each of us by the Holy Spirit who has been given to us.

Hope needs firmness to overcome difficulties, to keep peace and hand it on, and to go calmly to martyrdom. It has never been a virtue of the weak or a privilege of the hard-headed, the idle or the cowardly. Hope is strong, active and creative, it involves what is strenuous and difficult, even if possible (St Thomas). There is no such thing as hope for the easy or obvious. "Hope that is seen is not hope. For who hopes for what he sees? But if we hope for what we do not see, we wait for it with patience" (Rom 8:24-25). Difficult times require steadfastness in two senses: as firmness, constancy and perseverance, and as active, bold and creative commitment. To change the world with the spirit of the Beatitudes, and to build it up in peace, there is need of steadfastness in the Spirit. "You shall receive power when the Holy Spirit has come upon you; and you shall be my witnesses" (Rom 1:8). The first condition for a witness of Easter, that is of hope, is contemplation: to have heard and seen, to have touched the word of life (1 Jn 1:1-5); the second is the cross: to share deeply in the Lord's death and resurrection (Rom 6:3-6);

the third is steadfastness: the ability to go readily and gladly to martyrdom.

In difficult times there is an easy temptation against hope; it is to allow oneself to think of the past and to dream idly that the storm will soon pass without our doing anything to create the new times. Hope is an essentially creative virtue; so it will come to an end when, finally, everything is done and achieved. Heaven will be the rest following upon the searching of faith, the constancy of hope and the activity of love (1 Thess 1:3). Eternal happiness will be this: savouring in God for ever the Good perceived by faith, pursued in hope and attained in love.

But steadfastness is neither domination nor aggression. There are peoples who own nothing and hope for everything, and they are blissfully happy — because they are providentially strong in spirit. They possess God and enjoy his adorable presence in the silence of the cross. To be a man or woman of peace it is necessary to be strong. Only those who possess the strength of the Spirit can become peace-makers (Mt 5:5).

Strength is also necessary for embracing the cross with joy as the great gift of the Father, who is preparing fruit for the new age. There is a way of bearing the cross with affliction, resentment or sadness; then it wounds us. But it is inevitable in our lives and, for Christians, an essential condition of the following of Jesus. We were made for the cross, but we must embrace it before we can enter into glory (Lk 24:26). There are privileged souls who suffer much; but their great privilege is the cross. Their friends, as in the case of Job, try to avoid it — and so did Peter, when he did not understand the announcement of the Passion (Mt 16:22) — or as in the crucifixion of the Lord when the Jews asked him to come down from the cross so that they might believe in him. Today we are readier to believe in a person who speaks to us about the cross in cheerful and hopeful language, for his testimony is born of a profound experience of God.

A people who suffers can fall into passive and fatalist

resignation or into aggressive violence. We need therefore to love it with the strength of the Spirit to bring it into the way of hope. Also it may seem that the promised land is a long way off and that the hope of the prophets who proclaim chastisement and require penitence is a useless illusion. How can they speak of hope when so many children are dying of hunger every day and so many peoples suffer wretchedness and oppression? How speak of hope when there is so much injustice, so many lying accusations, kidnappings, imprisonments and deaths? How can we speak of hope when the church is wounded from within, and the authority of the pope and bishops is challenged?

Yet we must speak of hope, without doubt, and pass it on to the brethren, since when true Christians feel the essence of their own loyalty to the word, they really believe in God who never deceives, and experience the pain of the cross. Men and women have a right to see that we hope against all hope and that we are positive makers of peace, transmitters of joy and true prophets of hope.

We need to be ready for martyrdom. There was a time when we read the acts of the martyrs with veneration, and it was a story which moved us and filled us with courage. Today, anyone who decides to live on the basis of the gospel, must prepare himself for martyrdom. The worst is that in many cases stoning and killing is "in the name of Christ". That is the fulfilment of the Lord's word: "I have said all this to you to keep you from falling away … . Indeed the hour is coming when whoever kills you will think that he is offering service to God. And they will do this because they have not known the Father nor me. But I have said these things to you, that when their hour comes you may remember that I told you of them" (Jn 16:1-4). For this readiness for martyrdom the strength of the Spirit is, above all, needed. Jesus promised the Spirit to his apostles so that they might preach "with power", as the fruit of a palpable and enjoyable experience or contemplation, and go joyfully to martyrdom.

Here we are at the very heart of the gospel. Jesus was rejected, persecuted and vilified, imprisoned, crucified and led to his death. So were the apostles. But it was with joy that they took their part in the cross of Christ and with tranquillity that they prepared themselves for martyrdom. "They left the presence of the council, rejoicing that they were counted worthy to suffer dishonour for the name (of Jesus)" (Acts 5:41). Paul continued to preach even in prison; his great title is this: "I, the prisoner of Christ" (Eph 4:1). There is in the Acts a very beautiful passage, gentle and strong at the same time, which reveals to us Paul's deep and joyful readiness for martyrdom; it is when he is taking leave of the elders of Ephesus: "And now, behold, I am going up to Jerusalem, bound in the Spirit, not knowing what shall befall me there: except that the Holy Spirit testifies to me in every city that imprisonment and afflictions await me" (Acts 20:22-23). Yet Paul feels himself immensely happy — it is the only thing he minds about — at being faithful to the ministry he had received of bearing witness to the gospel of the grace of God.

Today, people, christian communities, and nations are suffering martyrdom. There is an easy and dangerous temptation to treat the gospel as politics, but there is also appearing a wish to reduce the gospel to silence and to lock it away among abstract schemes. It is easy to accept a gospel which proclaims the coming of Jesus in time and predicts his return, but vexation is the answer to a gospel which says that Jesus continues to live with us till the end of the world and demands of us a daily effort and righteousness, fraternal love, sacrifice to the Father and service to the brethren. "The church has the task of proclaiming the liberation of millions of human beings, of helping to bring about this liberation, of bearing witness of the same, and of seeing that it is really complete. All that is not foreign to evangelisation" (EN 30).

Everything which brings us to the evangelical obligation of Christianity, to the glorification of the Father, and to being servants of our fellows and builders of history is considered to be dangerous and subversive; and without doubt the gospel has something to say in all this and must be a leaven of peace and salvation for the existing world of history — the economic and social order and the political order — in which men and women move. It is necessary to be steadfast if one is to be faithful to the whole of the gospel.

Finally, there is something which requires particular steadfastness; it is keeping the balance of the Spirit for difficult times. It may be for us the risk of falling into indifference, hardness of heart or fear. There may also be the risk of our allowing ourselves to be carried away by the blizzard or by the easy euphoria of immediate results, of not wishing to change anything, so as not to disturb order or lose unity, or of trying to change everything from without or suddenly.

One of the fundamental characteristics of the new age — perhaps the first, according to Vatican II and Medellin — is change. Changes are speeded up, deep and universal. Precisely because of this the new age at once becomes a difficult age. To change everything from within, with the light of the Word and the action of the Spirit, is not easy. Change is not just replacing one thing by another, much less is it the quick destruction of what is ancient. Change is creation and growth; that is, from the wealth of the ancient we undertake the creation of the present and the preparation of the future. Difficult times may result in loss of balance, but loss of balance increases the difficulty of the new age, for there is a loss of inner serenity, of the far-sightedness of the contemplative and the creative bold-ness of the person of the Spirit. When balance is lacking, then passive fear or aggressive violence increases. Difficult times require strong men and women to live in the firm-ness and perseverance of hope. For this purpose there is a need of poor, contemplative men and women, totally divested of personal security so that they trust in God alone, and with a great capacity for discovering every day the Lord's passage in history, and for gladly dedicating themselves to the service of their fellows in the building up of a more fraternal and christian world. That means that we need "new men and women", able to appreciate the cross and to pass on the joy of the resurrection, able to love God above all things and their neighbour as themselves, able to experience the nearness of Jesus and to flood the world with hope. They must be capable of experiencing the "Lord who is at hand" (Phil 4:4), and therefore they are imperturbably cheerful, and of crying to their fellows that "the Lord comes" (cf. 1 Thess 16:22), and therefore they live in uncollapsible solidity of hope.

These are persons who have experienced God in the desert and have learnt to appreciate the cross. Therefore they can read the signs of the times by night, have made up their minds to give their lives for their friends, and, above all, count themselves happy to suffer for the name of Jesus and to share so deeply in the mystery of his Easter. For, in fidelity to the Word, they have understood that difficult times are the most providential and evangelical, and that they must be lived through in depth of contemplation and in the serenity of the cross. Thence arises the victory of faith in the world (1 Jn 5:4) and for all it becomes a fountain of peace, joy and hope.

Conclusion

"When the time had fully come, God sent forth his Son, born of a woman, born under the law, to redeem those who were under the law, that we might receive adoption as sons" (Gal 4:4-7).

The gospel "fullness" of difficult times was marked by the presence of Mary, "of whom Jesus was born, who is called Christ" (Mt 1:16). When difficult times burst into history by reason of the creatures' sin, Mary most holy was announced prophetically (Gen 3:15) as sharer in the salvation of humanity. When, "full of grace" (Lk 1:28), she said her "Yes", difficult times were changed into times of salvation. There were to continue to be difficult times, even more when marked with the cross than before: "He will be a sign that is spoken against (and a sword will pierce through your own soul also)" (Lk 2:34-35), but they were not to be impossible, because "with God nothing will be impossible" (Lk 1:37). Then began the change from sorrow into joy, from anxiety into calm, from desperation into hope. The three sentences of the angel of the Annunciation to Mary are significant: "Rejoice", "Do not be afraid", "For with God nothing will be impossible". God's profound invitation to joy, calmness and hope continues in history.

What will the new times which the Spirit has reserved for us be like? What will the new times which we ourselves, as instruments of the Spirit, are preparing for the future be like? All depends on God's plan, discovered in contemplation, accepted in poverty and realised in the strength of readiness for his service. Mary is with us. Certainly there are moments which are hard and difficult, yet clearly providential and fruitful, lovely moments of extraordinary grace, though humanly absurd and impossible. Yet what is impossible for the human person is made possible by God: Jesus assured us of this with these words: "With men this is impossible, but with God all things are possible" (Mt 19:26). God showed this to Abram (Gen 18:14) and repeated it to Mary (Lk 1:37). Job also understood it in his fruitful experience of pain, and he showed it in his last answer to the Lord: "I know that thou canst do all things, and that no purpose of thine can be thwarted" (Job 42:2).

All we need to do is to live in hope; and, for this very reason, in poverty, in contemplation and in the power of the Spirit, or, more concretely still, in the humble, joyful and total readiness of Mary, the faithful Virgin, who said "Yes" to the Father, and changed the world. And so she is now, in the light of the Spirit and as Mother of the Saviour, the Cause of joy and the Mother of Holy Hope for us. In Mary and with Mary, the church, which hears the word of God in poverty and keeps it (Lk 11:28), lives, silent and strong, at the foot of the paschal cross of Jesus (Jn 19:25), and very happily sings of the fidelity of a God who always continues to work wonders in the poverty of his servants, while she awaits in a vigil of prayer the Lord who is at hand (Mt 25:6). "Surely I am coming soon. Amen! Come, Lord Jesus" (Rev 22:20).